Mushroom Cookbook

An Easy Mushroom Cookbook with Delicious Mushroom Recipes

By
BookSumo Press
All rights reserved

Published by
http://www.booksumo.com

Table of Contents

Vito's Award Winning Linguine 7

Italian Mozzarella and Bacon Stuffed Mushrooms 8

Simple Japanese Stir-Fried Mushrooms 9

4-Ingredient Stuffed White Buttons 10

How to Fry Mushrooms 11

New England Style Stuffed Mushrooms 12

Sandra's Salisbury Steak 13

Stir Fried Mushrooms for Topping 15

German Egg Noodle and Chuck Dinner 16

Cube Steak Clásico 17

Dijon Chicken 18

Creamy Portabella Soup 19

Chicken with Mushroom and Thyme Sauce 20

Mushroom Lasagna 21

Central European Style Mushroom Soup 22

Monday's Mushroom Stir Fry 23

Vermont Soup 24

Parmesan Stuffed Mushroom Bites 25

Bella Burgers 26

Easy Chicken 27

Garden Party Mushroom Griller 28

Alternative Gratin 29

6-Ingredient Mushrooms Greek Style 30

Seattle Style Asparagus Skillet 31

Roasted Vegetable Sampler 32

Handmade Stuffing 33

Tennessee Style Chicken Breast 34

30-Minute Mushroom Rotini 35

Italian Seasoned Buttons 36

Alaskan Trout Dinner 37

Grilled Mushroom Parcel 38

Bell Mushroom Steak Sandwich 39

Chinese Mushroom Saucepan 40

Full Vegetarian Stroganoff 41

Tuesday's Dinner 42

Parmesan Mushroom Breakfast 43

Florida Style Stuffed Mushroom with Shrimp Cream 44

Herbed Sautéed Mushroom Caps 45

Asian-Fusion Ginger Mushroom 46

Full Fall Pot Roast 47

Saucy Red Button Skillet 48

Roasted Honey Mushroom Chicken 49

California Pizza Pan 50

Grated Spud and Mushroom Frittata 51

Thursday Morning Omelet 52

Tortellini Soup Toscano 53

Herbed Mushroom Cakes 54

Steak and Potato Dump Dinner with Gravy 55

Baja Mushroom Quesadillas 56

Creamy Weekend Fettuccine 57

Baked Rice 58

Pennsylvania Inspired Cabbage Skillet 59

Brooke's Burgers 60

Mushroom Loaves 61

Maylene's Stuffed Mushrooms 62

Potato Pierogis with Saucy Mushrooms 63

Heirloom Crepes 64

Handmade Cheese Raviolis 65

Mushroom Stir Fry 101 67

Garlicky Mushroom Skillet with Peas 68

How to Make Orzo 69

Friday Night Linguine 70

Broiled Halibut with Mushroom Salsa 71

Ontario Casserole 72

Extra Cheesy Mushroom Pizza 73

Simple Miso Soup 74

Maria's Quesadilla 75

Veal Cuts with Mushroom Sauce 76

Mushroom Pesto Spaghetti 77

Classic Turkey and Parsley Sauce 78

Balsamic Mushroom Buttons 79

True Country Pilaf 80

Mushroom Wellington 81

Pan Fried Tofu with Mushroom Gravy 83

How to Make Mushroom Pâté 84

Sesame Mushroom Stir Fry 85

Classic Piccata Chicken with Linguine 86

Seattle Toast 87

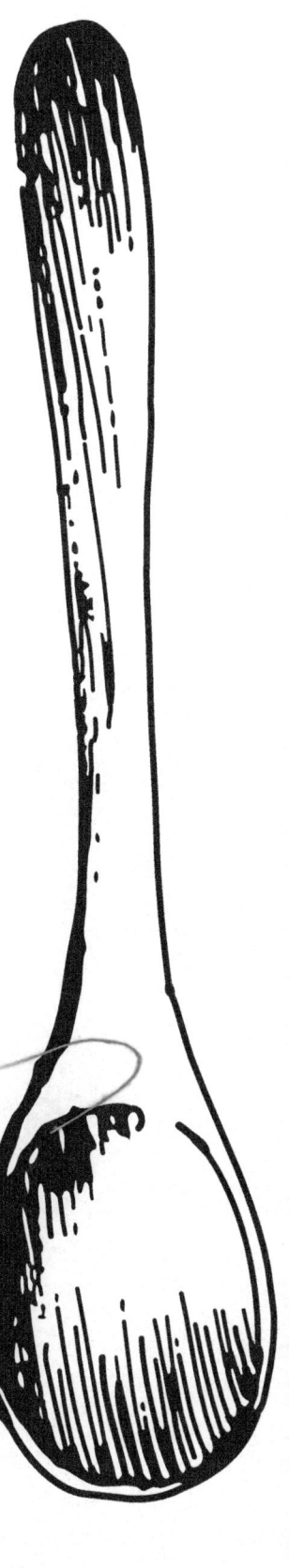

Creamy Mushroom Boursin 88

Twin Cities Style Pizzas 89

Country White Rice 90

Beef Stroganoff 91

Garden Portabella Turkey Burgers 92

Bangkok Chicken Pan 93

Vito's Award Winning Linguine

Prep Time: 10 mins
Total Time: 25 mins

Servings per Recipe: 4
Calories   670.7
Fat   26.1g
Cholesterol   45.8mg
Sodium   312.1mg
Carbohydrates   91.2g
Protein   18.8g

Ingredients

- 1 lb. linguine, cooked al dente, drain
- 6 tbsp butter
- 10 cloves garlic, minced
- 6 C. mushrooms, sliced
- 1 tsp dried basil
- 1/4 tsp salt
- pepper
- 2 tbsp olive oil
- 2 tbsp parsley, chopped
- parmesan cheese, grated

Directions

1. Prepare the pasta by following the instructions on the package.
2. Place a pan over medium heat. Heat in it 2 tbsp of butter. Cook in them the garlic with mushroom, basil, a pinch of salt and pepper.
3. Let them cook for 6 to 8 min until they become soft. Stir in the olive oil with the rest of the butter.
4. Turn off the heat. Stir in the linguine. Serve it warm.
5. Enjoy.

ITALIAN
Mozzarella and Bacon Stuffed Mushrooms

Prep Time: 20 mins
Total Time: 30 mins

Servings per Recipe: 1	
Calories	18.3
Fat	1.0g
Cholesterol	2.9mg
Sodium	46.4mg
Carbohydrates	1.0g
Protein	1.2g

Ingredients

1 lb. mushroom
3 slices turkey bacon, chopped
1/2 C. chopped onion
1 clove garlic, chopped
1 C. shredded mozzarella cheese
1/2 C. soft breadcrumbs
1/4 tsp oregano
1/4 tsp salt

Directions

1. Before you do anything, preheat the oven to 375 F.
2. Cut off the mushroom stems and chop them. Place the mushroom caps aside.
3. Place a pan over medium heat. Heat in it a splash of oil.
4. Cook in it the garlic with onion, mushroom stems, bacon, a pinch of salt and pepper.
5. Let them cook for 6 min. Add the rest of the ingredients. Let them cook to make the filling.
6. Spoon the filling into the mushroom caps. Place them on a baking sheet.
7. Place the pan in the oven and let them cook for 11 min.
8. Sprinkle some cheese on top then cook them for an extra 2 min.
9. Serve your cheesy mushroom caps warm.
10. Enjoy.

Simple
Japanese Stir-Fried Mushrooms

Prep Time: 10 mins
Total Time: 30 mins

Servings per Recipe: 4
Calories   76.0
Fat   3.4g
Cholesterol   7.6mg
Sodium   1039.6mg
Carbohydrates   7.0g
Protein   7.2g

Ingredients

1 tbsp butter
2 cloves garlic, minced
1 1/2 lbs. mushrooms, sliced
1/4 C. soy sauce
garlic powder

black pepper

Directions

1. Get a mixing bowl: Heat in it the butter until it melts.
2. Sauté in it the garlic for 2 to 3 min. Stir in the mushroom and cook them for 5 min.
3. Add the soy sauce with garlic powder, a pinch of salt and pepper. Let them cook for 11 min.
4. Serve your mushroom stir fry warm with some rice.
5. Enjoy.

4-INGREDIENT Stuffed White Buttons

Prep Time: 30 mins
Total Time: 1 hr 10 mins

Servings per Recipe: 6
Calories 343.2
Fat 31.8g
Cholesterol 83.9mg
Sodium 539.1mg
Carbohydrates 6.1g
Protein 10.3g

Ingredients

2 (12 oz.) packages white button mushrooms
1 (8 oz.) packages cream cheese
1 (8 oz.) packages beef sausage

1/4 C. butter

Directions

1. Before you do anything, preheat the oven to 350 F.
2. Clean the mushroom and rinse them. Drain them and cut of the stems. Chop the mushroom caps and place them aside.
3. Place a pan over medium heat. Cook in it the beef sausage for 5 min. Stir in the chopped stems with garlic.
4. Let them cook for 3 min. discard the excess fat.
5. Get a mixing bowl: Stir in it the cream cheese with the sausage mixture to make the filling.
6. Grease a baking dish with some batter. Place in it the mushroom caps with the hollow side facing up.
7. Spoon the spoon the filling into the caps. Pour some water on the side enough to cover the base of the pan.
8. Place it in the oven and let it cook for 32 to 46 min. Serve you mushroom casserole warm.
9. Enjoy.

How to Fry Mushrooms

Prep Time: 15 mins
Total Time: 25 mins

Servings per Recipe: 3
Calories	538.8
Fat	4.5g
Cholesterol	0.0mg
Sodium	821.4mg
Carbohydrates	106.4g
Protein	16.9g

Ingredients

10 oz. white mushrooms, wiped clean
1 C. flour
1/2 C. cornstarch
3/4 tsp baking powder
1/4 tsp salt
1 C. water
2 C. breadcrumbs

Directions

1. Get a mixing bowl: Stir in it the flour, cornstarch, baking powder and salt.
2. Pour in the water and whisk them until no lumps are found.
3. Place a deep pan over medium heat. Heat in it about 1/2 inch of oil.
4. Stick a toothpick into a mushroom. Dip it in the flour batter then roll it in the breadcrumbs.
5. Repeat the process with several other mushrooms then cook them in the hot oil until they become golden brown.
6. Drain the fried mushrooms and place them aside. Repeat the process with the remaining mushrooms.
7. Serve them with your favorite dip.
8. Enjoy.

NEW ENGLAND STYLE
Stuffed Mushrooms

Prep Time: 30 mins
Total Time: 50 mins

Servings per Recipe: 1
Calories 133.9
Fat 10.1g
Cholesterol 34.8mg
Sodium 357.2mg
Carbohydrates 2.4g
Protein 8.6g

Ingredients

1/4 C. olive oil
24 large white mushrooms
12 oz. flaked crabmeat
4 tbsp chopped onions
1 tsp dry mustard
1 C. shredded parmesan cheese
1 C. soft breadcrumbs
2 tsp parsley, chopped
1/8 tsp ground red pepper

1/8 tsp black pepper
1/8 tsp garlic salt
1 egg, beaten
3 tbsp mayonnaise
1/2 C. melted butter
1/4 tsp garlic salt
2 C. shredded parmesan cheese

Directions

1. Before you do anything, preheat the oven to 350 F. Grease a baking dish with some butter. Place it aside.
2. Clean the mushrooms, rinse them and dry them. Cut off the mushroom stems and chop them.
3. Get a mixing bowl: Place in it the chopped stems with crabmeat, onion, mustard, 1 C. parmesan cheese, soft bread crumbs, parsley, red and black pepper, and 1/8 tsp garlic salt.
4. Add the egg with mayo and combine them well to make the filling.
5. Place the mushroom caps in the greased dish. Spoon the filling into the mushroom caps.
6. Place the small pan over medium heat. Stir in it the butter with 1/4 tsp garlic salt until they melt.
7. Drizzle the mixture all over the stuffed mushroom caps. Sprinkle the remaining cheese on top.
8. Place the stuffed mushroom dish in the oven. Let it cook for 22 to 26 min. Serve it warm. Enjoy.

Sandra's Salisbury Steak

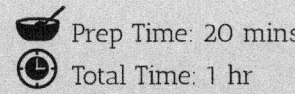
Prep Time: 20 mins
Total Time: 1 hr

Servings per Recipe: 2
Calories	1132.2
Fat	85.1g
Cholesterol	44.2g
Sodium	1951.2mg
Carbohydrates	36.4g
Protein	56.1g

Ingredients

Steak
- 1 lb. ground beef
- 1/3 C. chopped onion
- 1/4 C. cracker crumb
- 1 egg, beaten
- 1 1/2 tbsp horseradish
- 1 tsp salt
- 1 tsp pepper
- 2 tbsp butter
- 1 medium onion, sliced into, rings
- 8 oz. fresh mushrooms, sliced
- 3 tbsp butter

Gravy
- 3 tbsp flour
- salt
- pepper
- 1/2 C. cream
- 3/4 C. chicken broth
- 1 dash Worcestershire sauce
- 1 dash hot sauce

Directions

1. Get a mixing bowl: Mix in it the ground beef, chopped onions, cracker crumbs, egg, horseradish, salt and pepper.
2. Form the mixture into 2 burgers.
3. Place a pan over medium heat. Heat in it 2 tbsp of butter until it melts. Add the burgers and let them cook for 9 min on each side.
4. Place a small pan over medium heat. Heat in it the remaining butter. Cook in it the onion with mushroom for 6 min.
5. Drain the steak burgers and place them aside. Mix the flour into the juices in the pan with a pinch of salt and pepper.
6. Let them cook for 2 to 3 min while stirring them all the time. Add the cream and stir them until they become thick.
7. Stir in the broth until you get a smooth sauce. Let it cook until it becomes slightly thick.
8. Stir in the Worcestershire sauce with hot sauce.

9. Stir in the mushroom and onion mix with the steak burgers. Let them cook for 12 min over low heat.
10. Serve your steak burgers with the mushroom gravy warm with some rice.
11. Get a mixing bowl:
12. Enjoy.

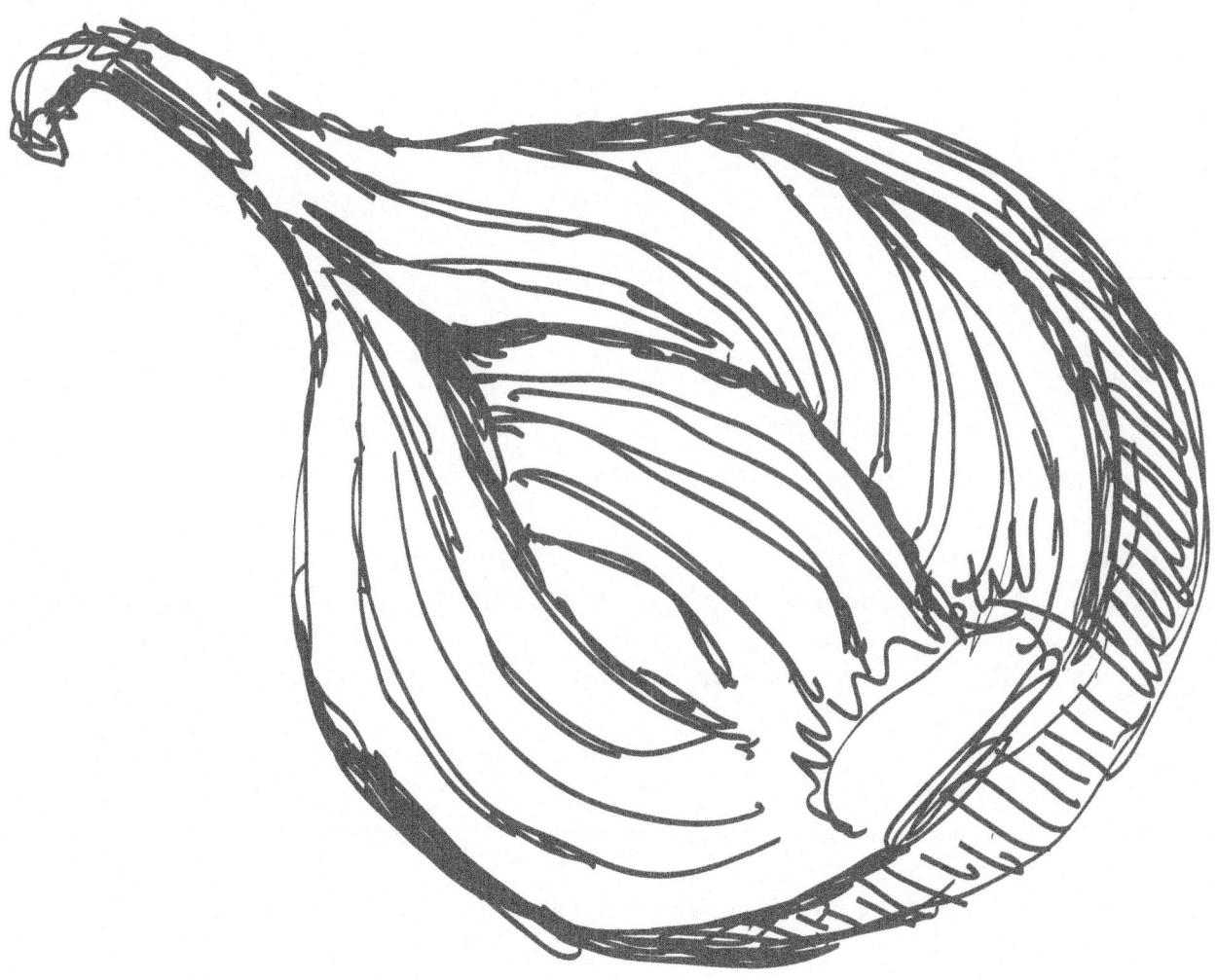

Stir Fried Mushrooms for Topping

Prep Time: 10 mins
Total Time: 40 mins

Servings per Recipe: 4
Calories   105.9
Fat   9.3g
Cholesterol   15.2mg
Sodium   68.7mg
Carbohydrates   4.8g
Protein   2.1g

Ingredients

- 1/2 lb. sliced mushrooms
- 1 medium onion, wedges
- 2 tbsp butter
- 1 tbsp olive oil
- 1 tsp Worcestershire sauce
- 1/4 tsp garlic salt

Directions

1. Place a pan over medium heat. Heat in it the oil with butter.
2. Stir in the onion with mushroom. Let them cook for 22 min until they become soft.
3. Stir in the Worcestershire sauce and garlic salt. Serve your stir fry warm with some grilled steaks.
4. Enjoy.

GERMAN
Egg Noodle and Chuck Dinner

 Prep Time: 15 mins
Total Time: 2 hrs 15 mins

Servings per Recipe: 10
Calories 911.2
Fat 29.6g
Cholesterol 313.3mg
Sodium 903.8mg
Carbohydrates 74.0g
Protein 87.7g

Ingredients

7 1/2-8 lbs. boneless beef chuck roast, cut into chunks
coarse ground black pepper
oil
1 (32 oz.) boxes beef broth
1 large onion sectioned and separated
1 (1 oz.) envelope French onion soup mix
1/4 C. A.1. Original Sauce
1 tbsp minced garlic
4 tbsp butter
salt
2 (8 oz.) containers sliced mushrooms
4 tbsp cornstarch
4 tbsp cold water
2 (16 oz.) bags frozen egg noodles, cooked and drained

Directions

1. Place a large pot over medium heat. Heat in it a splash of oil.
2. Cook in it the beef roast for 4 to 6 min on each side. Stir in the broth, onion, soup mix, A-1, garlic, butter and salt.
3. Let them cook for 100 min over low heat. Stir in the mushroom and let them cook for an extra 16 to 22 min.
4. Once the time is up, remove the cover.
5. Get a small mixing bowl: Whisk in it the cornstarch with water. Stir it into the pot. Let them cook for 6 min until the sauce becomes slightly thick. Stir in the noodles. Adjust the seasoning of your noodles stew then serve it warm.
6. Enjoy.

Cube Steak Clásico

Prep Time: 15 mins
Total Time: 30 mins

Servings per Recipe: 4
Calories   342.9
Fat   34.2g
Cholesterol   104.4mg
Sodium   1798.2mg
Carbohydrates   8.7g
Protein   3.5g

Ingredients

Steaks
4 cube steaks
3 - 4 tbsp cracked black pepper
1 tbsp kosher salt
1 tbsp olive oil
1 tbsp soft butter
Sauce
8 oz. cremini mushrooms, sliced
1 shallot, peeled and minced
2 garlic cloves, peeled and minced
1 tbsp basil, chopped
1 C. heavy cream
2 tbsp soft unsalted butter

Directions

1. For the meat:
2. Sprinkle some salt and pepper all over the steak cubes.
3. Place a pan over medium heat. Heat in it the oil. Cook in it the steak dices for 5 to 7 min while stirring them often.
4. Drain them and cover them with a piece of foil.
5. heat the rest of the butter in the same pan. Cook in it the mushroom and shallot for 5 min.
6. Add the garlic and cook them for 1 min. Stir in the cooked steak dices with cream. Let them cook until the cream reduce by 1/3.
7. Adjust the seasoning of your cream steak pan then serve it hot with noodles.
8. Enjoy.

DIJON Chicken

Prep Time: 15 mins
Total Time: 30 mins

Servings per Recipe: 4
Calories   307.3
Fat   18.8g
Cholesterol   102.9mg
Sodium   219.0mg
Carbohydrates   6.8g
Protein   27.2g

Ingredients

- 4 boneless skinless chicken breast halves
- 2 tbsp flour
- 2 tbsp vegetable oil
- 1 tbsp butter
- 1 small onion, chopped
- 1 C. mushroom, sliced
- 1/2 C. light cream
- 1 tbsp fresh parsley, chopped
- 1 tbsp Dijon mustard
- 1 tbsp lemon juice

Directions

1. Place the chicken breasts between 2 wax sheets. Use a kitchen hammer or pan to flatten them until they become 1/4 inch thick.
2. Season the chicken breasts with some salt and pepper. Dust them with flour.
3. Place a pan over medium heat. Heat in it the oil. Cook in it the chicken breasts for 7 to 9 min on each side.
4. Drain the chicken breasts and place them aside.
5. Heat the butter in the pan over high heat. Cook in it the mushroom with onion for 6 min.
6. Lower the heat. Stir in the cream with parsley, mustard and lemon juice.
7. Let them cook until they start boiling while stirring them often.
8. Transfer the chicken breasts into serving plates. Drizzle the mushroom sauce over then serve them hot.
9. Enjoy.

Creamy Portabella Soup

🥣 Prep Time: 10 mins
🕐 Total Time: 45 mins

Servings per Recipe: 8
Calories 223.8
Fat 18.0g
Cholesterol 56.0mg
Sodium 365.9mg
Carbohydrates 12.0g
Protein 5.8g

Ingredients

- 4 tbsp unsalted butter
- 2 leeks, halved lengthwise and sliced
- 1 large onion, chopped
- 3 large portabella mushrooms, dark gills scraped out, chopped
- 3 tbsp all-purpose flour
- 1 1/2 tsp dried thyme leaves
- 1 bay leaf
- 6 C. low sodium chicken broth
- 1 tsp salt
- 1 tsp sugar
- 1/2 tsp pepper
- 1 C. heavy cream
- 1/4 C. chopped parsley

Directions

1. Place a large pot over medium heat. Heat in it the butter. Cook in it the leeks with onion for 4 min.
2. Stir in the mushroom and let them cook for 11 min over low heat with the lid on.
3. Add the flour and cook them for 2 min over medium heat. Stir in the thyme, bay leaf, broth, salt, sugar, and pepper.
4. Put on half a cover then let them cook for 12 min.
5. Allow the soup to sit for few minutes. Discard the bay lead then use an immersion blender to blend it smooth.
6. Stir the cream into the soup with a pinch of salt and pepper. Heat it for few minutes then serve it warm.
7. Enjoy.

CHICKEN with Mushroom and Thyme Sauce

Prep Time: 5 mins
Total Time: 20 mins

Servings per Recipe: 4
Calories 523.1
Fat 37.5g
Cholesterol 187.5mg
Sodium 285.8mg
Carbohydrates 16.1g
Protein 32.4g

Ingredients

1/3 C. all-purpose flour
1 1/2 tsp dried thyme
1/2 tsp ground allspice
4 large boneless skinless chicken breast halves
1/4 C. butter
1 lb. mushroom, sliced
1 small onion, chopped
1 C. whipping cream
1 C. canned low sodium chicken broth

Directions

1. Before you do anything, preheat the oven to 350 F.
2. Get a mixing bowl: Combine in it the flour, 1/2 tsp thyme and allspice. Reserve 1 tbsp of it aside.
3. Season the chicken breasts with some salt and pepper. Dust them with the flour mix.
4. Place a pan over medium heat. Heat in it the butter. Cook in it the chicken over medium heat for 4 to 6 min on each side.
5. Once the time is up, drain the chicken breasts and place them aside.
6. Stir the mushrooms, onion, and remaining 1 tsp thyme into the same pan.
7. Let them cook for 6 min. Stir in the remaining 1 tbsp of the flour mix you put aside. Stir them for 1 min.
8. Stir into the broth with cream. Let them cook until they start boiling.
9. Stir the cooked chicken breasts back into the pan. Heat them for 6 min. Serve your creamy chicken and mushroom warm with some noodles or rice. Enjoy.

Mushroom Lasagna

Prep Time: 40 mins
Total Time: 1 hr 10 mins

Servings per Recipe: 8
Calories   288.5
Fat   11.7g
Cholesterol   62.0mg
Sodium   814.3mg
Carbohydrates   31.1g
Protein   16.6g

Ingredients

- 9 -10 lasagna noodles, uncooked
- 1 (14 oz.) cans diced tomatoes with juice, undrained
- 1 (8 oz.) cans tomato sauce
- 1 (6 oz.) cans tomato paste
- 1 tbsp balsamic vinegar
- 1 tbsp dried basil
- 1 tsp dried oregano
- 1/2-1 tsp garlic powder
- salt and pepper
- 2 C. shredded mozzarella cheese, divided
- 1 C. feta cheese, crumbled
- 1 (10 oz.) packages frozen chopped spinach, thawed and squeezed dry
- 1 egg, slightly beaten
- 1/2-1 lb. portabella mushroom, sliced

Directions

1. Before you do anything, preheat the oven to 350 F. Grease a casserole dish.
2. Prepare the noodles by following the instructions on the package.
3. Place a saucepan over medium heat. Combine in it the tomatoes (with juice), tomato sauce, tomato paste, vinegar and seasonings.
4. Bring them to a boil. Lower the heat and put on the lid. Let them cook for 22 to 26 min.
5. Pour 1/3 of the sauce into the greased pan and spread it in an even layer.
6. Cover it with 3 noodles sheets. Spread over them 1/2 of the cheese mix, 1/2 of the mushroom slices and 1/3 of the tomato sauce.
7. Repeat the process to make another layer ending with noodles and tomato sauce on top.
8. Sprinkle the mozzarella cheese over it. Lay a loose sheet of foil over the dish.
9. Place the lasagna in the oven and let it cook for 26 min.
10. Once the time is up, discard the foil and cook it for an extra 5 min. Serve it warm
11. Get a mixing bowl:
12. Enjoy.

CENTRAL EUROPEAN
Style Mushroom Soup

Prep Time: 20 mins
Total Time: 45 mins

Servings per Recipe: 4
Calories   226.9
Fat   14.3g
Cholesterol   38.7mg
Sodium   947.2mg
Carbohydrates   19.9g
Protein   7.6g

Ingredients

12 oz. mushrooms, -sliced
2 C. onions, chopped
2 tbsp butter
3 tbsp flour
1 C. milk
2 tsp dill weed
1 tbsp Hungarian paprika
1 tbsp tamari soy sauce
1 tsp salt
2 C. stock
2 tsp lemon juice
1/4 C. parsley, chopped
ground black pepper, -
1/2 C. sour cream

Directions

1. Place a soup pot over medium heat. Stir in it 2 tbsp of stock with onion and a pinch of salt.
2. Let them cook for 3 min. Stir in the mushroom with 1 tsp dill, 1/2 C. stock or water, soy sauce, and paprika.
3. Put on the lid and let them cook for 16 min over low heat.
4. Place a heavy saucepan over medium heat. Heat in it the butter until it melts.
5. Mix into it the flour and cook it for 2 min. Stir in the milk and whisk them until they become smooth for 11 min
6. Stir it into the soup pot with the rest of the stock. Put on the lid and let them cook for 12 to 16 min.
7. Stir in the lemon juice, sour cream and parsley.
8. Adjust the seasoning of your soup then serve it warm with your favorite toppings.
9. Enjoy.

Monday's Mushroom Stir Fry

Prep Time: 10 mins
Total Time: 25 mins

Servings per Recipe: 4
Calories   140.2
Fat   12.1g
Cholesterol   30.5mg
Sodium   183.4mg
Carbohydrates   6.6g
Protein   4.2g

Ingredients

- 1 lb. asparagus spear, trimmed
- 1/4 C. butter
- 2 C. mushrooms, sliced
- 2 tbsp Dijon mustard
- 1/4 tsp ground black pepper
- 1/2 tsp garlic, minced
- salt

Directions

1. Place a pan over medium heat. Lay in it the asparagus and cover it with water.
2. Bring them to a rolling boil for 6 to 8 min until they become tender.
3. Discard the water from the pan. Stir the rest of the ingredients into the asparagus.
4. Let them cook for 6 min. serve it warm.
5. Enjoy.

VERMONT
Soup

Prep Time: 20 mins
Total Time: 1 hr 50 mins

Servings per Recipe: 4
Calories 307.0
Fat 18.4g
Cholesterol 45.8mg
Sodium 1073.9mg
Carbohydrates 19.9g
Protein 7.6g

Ingredients

6 tbsp butter
2 C. -minced yellow onions
1/2 tsp sugar
1 lb. fresh mushrooms
1/4 C. flour
1 C. water
1 3/4 C. chicken broth
1 C. vegetable broth

1 tsp salt
1/2 tsp pepper
1 tsp thyme

Directions

1. Place a saucepan over medium heat. Heat in it the butter. Stir in the onions, sugar, and thyme. Let them cook for 35 min over low heat.
2. Stir in the mushroom and let them cook for 6 min.
3. Add the flour and mi them well. Let them cook for 3 min while always stirring them.
4. Stir in the remaining ingredients. Bring them to a boil. Lower the heat and let them cook for 14 min over low heat.
5. Adjust the seasoning of your soup then serve it warm.
6. Enjoy.

Parmesan Stuffed Mushroom Bites

Prep Time: 15 mins
Total Time: 45 mins

Servings per Recipe: 6
Calories   209.3
Fat   8.0g
Cholesterol   17.5mg
Sodium   370.4mg
Carbohydrates   25.5g
Protein   10.2g

Ingredients

- 24 large mushrooms, stems removed and stems chopped
- 2 tbsp butter
- 1 C. onion, diced
- 1/4 tsp dried thyme
- 1 1/2 C. spinach, chopped
- 3 tbsp breadcrumbs
- 1/2 C. parmesan cheese, grated
- salt and pepper

Directions

1. Before you do anything, preheat the oven to 350 F. Coat a baking sheet with 1 tbsp of butter.
2. Place a pan over medium heat. Heat in it the butter until it melts.
3. Cook in it the thyme with onion for 3 min.. Stir in the mushroom stems with spinach and breadcrumbs.
4. Let them cook for 6 min over high heat. Turn off the heat then stir it the parmesan cheese with a pinch of salt and pepper.
5. Place the mushroom caps on the greased sheet. Spoon the filling into them.
6. Dot them with the remaining butter. Place the sheet in the oven and let them cook for 16 to 21 min.
7. Serve your stuffed mushroom caps warm.
8. Enjoy.

BELLA
Burgers

Prep Time: 15 mins
Total Time: 35 mins

Servings per Recipe: 4
Calories 554.2
Fat 20.9g
Cholesterol 19.6mg
Sodium 801.9mg
Carbohydrates 76.3g
Protein 21.0g

Ingredients

4 large portabella mushrooms
1/4 C. balsamic vinegar
2 tbsp olive oil
1 tsp dried basil
1 tsp dried oregano
2 - 4 cloves garlic, minced
salt and pepper
4 oz. sliced provolone cheese

4 whole wheat rolls
sliced tomatoes
romaine lettuce leaf
sliced grilled onion
Dijon mustard

Directions

1. Cut off the mushroom stems and discard them.
2. Lay the mushroom caps on a lined up baking sheet with the smooth side facing up.
3. Season them with some salt and pepper.
4. Get a mixing bowl: Mix in it the vinegar, oil, basil, oregano, and garlic to make the marinade.
5. Drizzle it all over the mushroom caps. Let them sit for 12 to 16 min.
6. Before you do anything, preheat the grill and grease it.
7. Drain the mushroom caps and reserve the marinade. Place them over the grill.
8. Let the mushroom cook for 3 to 4 min on each side. Baste them with the reserved marinade every once in a while.
9. Lay on them the cheese slices and cook them for an extra minute.
10. Place the cheesy mushroom in a bread rolls with your favorite toppings and sauce.
11. Enjoy.

Easy Chicken

🥣 Prep Time: 20 mins
🕐 Total Time: 40 mins

Servings per Recipe: 2
Calories   739.6
Fat   46.0g
Cholesterol   207.2mg
Sodium   569.1mg
Carbohydrates   8.1g
Protein   61.7g

Ingredients

1 lb. boneless skinless chicken breast
kosher salt
pepper
3 tbsp olive oil
6 oz. cremini mushrooms, sliced
2 garlic cloves, minced
1/2 C. chicken broth
1/3 C. heavy cream
2 oz. crumbled gorgonzola
2 tbsp chopped Italian parsley

Directions

1. Cut the chicken breast into 3/4 inch slices. Sprinkle over them some salt and pepper.
2. Place a pan over medium heat. Heat in it 2 tbsp of oil. Cook in it half of the chicken slices for 2 to 3 min on each side.
3. Drain them and place them aside. Repeat the process with the remaining chicken slices.
4. Heat 1 tbsp of oil in the same pan. Cook in it the mushroom with a pinch of salt for 4 min.
5. Stir in the garlic and cook them for 1 min. Stir in the broth and let them cook for 2 to 3 min.
6. Add the cream and cook them for 2 min. Stir in 2/3 of the gorgonzola cheese. Stir them until they melt.
7. Adjust the seasoning of the sauce. Stir in the cooked chicken stripes and heat them for few minutes.
8. Garnish your creamy chicken and mushroom skillet with some parsley, and the remaining cheese.
9. Enjoy.

GARDEN PARTY
Mushroom Griller

Prep Time: 10 mins
Total Time: 25 mins

Servings per Recipe: 4
Calories   64.5
Fat   5.8g
Cholesterol   0.0mg
Sodium   69.6mg
Carbohydrates   2.2g
Protein   1.8g

Ingredients

1/2 lb. whole mushrooms
1/4 C. margarine, melted
1/2 tsp dill weed

1/2 tsp garlic salt

Directions

1. Before you do anything, preheat the grill and grease it.
2. Get a mixing bowl: Mix in it the margarine, dill, and garlic salt.
3. Stick the mushroom into skewers. Coat them with the margarine mix.
4. Place the mushroom skewers on the grill. Cook them for 5 to 6 min.
5. Serve them warm with some sour cream.
6. Enjoy.

Alternative Gratin

Prep Time: 10 mins
Total Time: 20 mins

Servings per Recipe: 4
Calories   328.1
Fat   26.1g
Cholesterol   72.5mg
Sodium   321.4mg
Carbohydrates 12.9g
Protein   14.7g

Ingredients

- 1/4 C. butter
- 2 lbs. mushrooms, sliced
- 3 garlic cloves, minced
- 2/3 C. sour cream
- salt and pepper
- 2 tbsp all-purpose flour
- 1/4 C. chopped parsley
- 1 C. shredded mozzarella cheese

Directions

1. Before you do anything, preheat the oven to 400 F. Coat a casserole dish with a cooking spray.
2. Place a pan over medium heat. Heat in it the butter. Cook in it the mushroom for 4 min.
3. Add the garlic and cook them for 1 min.
4. Get a mixing bowl: Mix in it the sour cream with flour, a pinch of salt and pepper.
5. Stir it into the mushroom. Cook them until they start boiling.
6. Spoon the mixture into the greased dish. Top it with shredded mozzarella and parsley.
7. Place the casserole in the oven and let it cook for 12 to 16 min.
8. Serve it warm with some rice or noodles.
9. Enjoy.

6-INGREDIENT
Mushrooms Greek Style

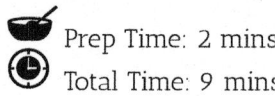

Prep Time: 2 mins
Total Time: 9 mins

Servings per Recipe: 4
Calories 155.2
Fat 13.9g
Cholesterol 0.0mg
Sodium 590.1mg
Carbohydrates 5.8g
Protein 3.5g

Ingredients

1/4 C. olive oil
1 lb. white mushroom, halved
3 tbsp balsamic vinegar
1 tsp salt

1/4 tsp red pepper flakes
pepper

Directions

1. Place a pan over medium heat. Heat in it the oil. Cook in it the mushroom for 5 to 6 min.
2. Add the vinegar, red pepper flakes salt and a pinch of pepper. Let them cook for 1 min.
3. Serve your mushroom warm with as a side dish or a sandwich topping.
4. Enjoy.

Seattle Style Asparagus Skillet

Prep Time: 10 mins
Total Time: 20 mins

Servings per Recipe: 2
Calories	200.9
Fat	17.7g
Cholesterol	45.8mg
Sodium	174.3mg
Carbohydrates	8.9g
Protein	5.2g

Ingredients

- 1/2 small onion, sliced
- 1 1/2 C. mushrooms, sliced
- 1 1/2 C. asparagus, chopped tips and most tender parts
- 3 - 4 tbsp butter
- salt and pepper

Directions

1. Place a pan over medium heat. Heat in it the butter. Sauté in it the onion for 3 min.
2. Stir in the mushroom and let it cook for 3 min. Stir in the asparagus with a pinch of salt and pepper.
3. Let them cook for 3 to 4 min. Serve it warm.
4. Enjoy.

ROASTED Vegetable Sampler

Prep Time: 5 mins
Total Time: 30 mins

Servings per Recipe: 4
Calories   61.6
Fat   2.8g
Cholesterol   0.0mg
Sodium   159.5mg
Carbohydrates   8.0g
Protein   2.8g

Ingredients

3 medium zucchini, halved lengthwise and sliced
1 1/2 C. sliced mushrooms
1 yellow onion, sliced and separated into rings

2 - 3 tsp extra virgin olive oil
1/4 tsp salt
1/2 tsp dried Italian seasoning

Directions

1. Before you do anything, preheat the oven to 450 F.
2. Get a mixing bowl: Stir in it all the ingredients.
3. Transfer them to a roasting tray and spray in an even layer.
4. Place it in the oven and let them cook for 16 min.
5. Toss the veggies and let them cook for an extra 8 min. Serve them warm.
6. Enjoy.

Handmade Stuffing

Prep Time: 30 mins
Total Time: 1 hr 30 mins

Servings per Recipe: 6
Calories   271.4
Fat   22.4g
Cholesterol   40.6mg
Sodium   457.0mg
Carbohydrates   15.1g
Protein   5.1g

Ingredients

- 1/2 C. uncooked wild rice
- 4 C. cubed day-old French bread
- 1/2 C. butter
- 1 large onion, chopped
- 1 garlic clove, minced
- 3 C. fresh mushrooms, sliced
- 1/2 tsp sage
- 1/2 tsp dried thyme leaves, crushed
- 1/2 tsp salt
- 1/4 tsp black pepper
- 1 C. chicken broth, from giblet boil
- 1/2 C. chopped pecans

Directions

1. Prepare the rice by following the instructions on the package.
2. Before you do anything, preheat the oven to 350 F.
3. Lay the bread cubes on a lined up baking sheet. Place it 5 inches away from the heat source.
4. Let them cook for 2 min. Place them aside to cool down.
5. Place a pan over medium heat. Heat in it the butter. Cook in it the garlic with onion for 4 min.
6. Stir in the mushroom and cook them for another 4 min. Stir in the sage with thyme, a pinch of salt and pepper.
7. Let them cook for 1 min. Add the broth with pecans and bread cubes.
8. Transfer the mixture to a greased casserole dish. Cover it with piece of foil.
9. Place it in the oven and let it cook for 42 min.
10. Serve your stuffing warm with some turkey or chicken roast.
11. Enjoy.

TENNESSEE STYLE
Chicken Breast

Prep Time: 15 mins
Total Time: 42 mins

Servings per Recipe: 4
Calories 314.0
Fat 16.4g
Cholesterol 113.1mg
Sodium 639.3mg
Carbohydrates 7.7g
Protein 32.5g

Ingredients

4 large boneless skinless chicken breasts
1/4 C. flour
3 tbsp butter
1 C. mushroom, sliced
1/2 C. chicken broth
1/4 tsp salt
1/8 tsp pepper

1/3 C. mozzarella cheese
1/3 C. parmesan cheese
1/4 C. green onion, sliced

Directions

1. Season the chicken breasts with some salt and pepper. Dust them with flour.
2. Before you do anything, preheat the oven to 350 F.
3. Place a pan over medium heat. Heat in it the butter. Cook in it the chicken breasts for 3 to 5 min on each side.
4. Drain them and place them on a baking sheet.
5. Cook the mushroom in the same pan for 3 min. Stir in the broth with a pinch of salt and pepper.
6. Cook them until they start boiling. Keep them cooking for 6 min.
7. Pour the mushroom mixture over the chicken breasts. Place them in the oven and let them cook for 16 min.
8. Once the time is up, top them with cheese and green onions.
9. Cook them for an extra 6 min in the oven. Serve them warm.
10. Enjoy.

30-Minute Mushroom Rotini

🥣 Prep Time: 15 mins
🕐 Total Time: 23 mins

Servings per Recipe: 4
Calories   477.1
Fat   9.5g
Cholesterol   17.0mg
Sodium   664.0mg
Carbohydrates   79.6g
Protein   18.8g

Ingredients

- 12 oz. rotini noodles
- 1 tbsp olive oil
- 3 cloves garlic, minced
- 1 C. onion, chopped
- 1 tbsp thyme
- 4 C. mixed mushrooms, sliced
- 2 tbsp all-purpose flour
- 2 C. milk
- 2 C. spinach, rinsed well & chopped
- 1/2 C. basil, chopped
- 1 tsp salt
- ground pepper
- grated parmesan cheese

Directions

1. Place a skillet over medium heat. Heat in it the oil. Sauté in it the thyme with onion and garlic for 2 min.
2. Stir in the mushroom and cook them for 7 to 9 min.
3. Add the flour and mix them for 1 min while cooking. Stir in the milk gradually.
4. Let them cook until they start boiling. Let them cook for 3 min stirring them all the time until they become thick.
5. Add the spinach with basil, a pinch of salt and pepper. Cook them for 4 min.
6. Serve your creamy mushroom and spinach skillet with some noodles.
7. Enjoy.

ITALIAN
Seasoned Buttons

Prep Time: 15 mins
Total Time: 30 mins

Servings per Recipe: 4
Calories   151.5
Fat   15.3g
Cholesterol   40.0mg
Sodium   137.7mg
Carbohydrates   2.8g
Protein   2.3g

Ingredients

3 oz. butter
2 garlic cloves, crushed
13 oz. button mushrooms, wiped clean
salt
black pepper

1/4 tsp cayenne pepper
2 tbsp parsley, chopped
1 tbsp basil, chopped
bread, assorted crusty

Directions

1. Place a pan over medium heat. Heat in it the butter. Sauté in it the garlic for 1 min.
2. Stir in the mushroom. Cook them for 5 min over high heat.
3. Stir in the cayenne, parsley, basil, a pinch of salt and pepper. Let them cook for 2 min.
4. Serve your herbed mushroom skillet warm as a side dish or a topping.
5. Enjoy.

Alaskan Trout Dinner

Prep Time: 5 mins
Total Time: 32 mins

Servings per Recipe: 5
Calories   825.8
Fat   53.8g
Cholesterol   221.6mg
Sodium   304.0mg
Carbohydrates   10.5g
Protein   73.6g

Ingredients

5 (3/4 lb.) trout, cleaned and dried
1/2 C. olive oil
5 cloves garlic, chopped
ground black pepper
salt
1/2 - 3/4 lb. mushrooms
1/4 - 1/2 C. butter
4 tbsp fine dry breadcrumbs

4 green onions, sliced
3 fresh lemons
2 tbsp minced parsley

Directions

1. Before you do anything, preheat the oven to 350 F.
2. Brush the whole trout with some olive oil. Season it with some salt and pepper.
3. Lay half of the mushroom slices in the bottom of a casserole dish. Top it with the trout fish.
4. Sprinkle the bread crumbs over it followed by the parsley garlic and green onion.
5. Play a small pan over medium heat. Heat in it the butter with olive oil and the juice of 2 lemons.
6. Drizzle the mixture over the trout fish. Place it in the oven and let it cook for 22 to 26 min.
7. Place a skillet over medium heat. Heat in it some butter. Cook in it the remaining mushroom for 3min.
8. Lay it over the baked trout fish then serve it warm with some rice.
9. Enjoy.

GRILLED
Mushroom Parcel

Prep Time: 15 mins
Total Time: 15 mins

Servings per Recipe: 4
Calories 51.0
Fat 2.1g
Cholesterol 0.0mg
Sodium 9.4mg
Carbohydrates 6.5g
Protein 4.0g

Ingredients

1 lemon
1 tbsp dried parsley
1/2 tbsp olive oil
3 garlic cloves, minced
2 green onions, chopped
1 lb. mushroom, cleaned
salt and pepper,

Directions

1. Before you do anything, preheat the grill and grease it.
2. Place the mushroom in a large piece of oil. Crumble the sides to prevent the juices from spilling.
3. Add to it the lemon juice and zest with the remaining ingredients. Toss them to coat.
4. Place the mushroom parcel over the grill. Let it cook for 7 to 8 min.
5. Serve it warm as a side dish or topping.
6. Enjoy.

Bell Mushroom Steak Sandwich

🍲 Prep Time: 45 mins
🕒 Total Time: 45 mins

Servings per Recipe: 4
Calories   699.1
Fat   27.4g
Cholesterol   120.2mg
Sodium   1063.5mg
Carbohydrates   66.8g
Protein   47.0g

Ingredients

- 2 onions, sliced
- 2 tbsp butter
- 2 tbsp oil
- 1 lb. white button mushrooms, sliced
- 2 tbsp minced garlic
- 1 C. beef broth
- 3 tbsp whipping cream
- 3 tbsp ketchup
- 1 tbsp Worcestershire sauce
- 2 tsp Dijon mustard
- 1 lb. cooked leftover steak
- salt and pepper
- 1 large green bell pepper, seeded and sliced
- sliced mozzarella cheese
- 1 loaf unsliced bread halved lengthwise

Directions

1. Before you do anything, preheat the oven broiler.
2. Coat each bread half with butter. Broil the bread for 2 to 4 min until it becomes crisp. Place a pan over medium heat. Heat in it the oil. Cook in it the onion with a pinch of salt and pepper for 4 min
3. Stir in mushroom with garlic. Cook them for 4 min. Add more butter or oil if needed. Drain the mushroom mix and place it aside.
4. Stir the beef broth with Worcestershire sauce and black pepper into the same pan.
5. Heat them for 3 min. Stir in the whipping cream, ketchup and mustard. Let them cook for another 3 min over low heat. Stir in the mushroom mixture with beef slices. Let them cook for 4 min over low heat.
6. Lay the bottom half of the bread on a large plate. Lay over it some cheese slices.
7. Top it with the steak and mushroom mixture. Lay over it the bell pepper slices, followed some extra cheese slices.
8. Cover them with the top bread half. Slice the sandwich into serving slices then serve them right away. Enjoy.

CHINESE Mushroom Saucepan

Prep Time: 5 mins
Total Time: 25 mins

Servings per Recipe: 8
Calories 77.4
Fat 6.9g
Cholesterol 0.0mg
Sodium 254.5mg
Carbohydrates 2.5g
Protein 1.9g

Ingredients

1/8 C. extra virgin olive oil
1/8 C. sesame oil
1/4 C. white vinegar
2 tbsp soy sauce
2 tbsp chopped garlic
5 C. mushrooms
2 tbsp sliced green onions

Directions

1. Place a heavy saucepan over medium heat. Stir in it the oil, vinegar, soy sauce, garlic and mushrooms.
2. Cook them until they start boiling. Lower the heat and let them cook for an extra 16 min.
3. Drain the mushrooms and transfer them to a serving plate.
4. Garnish them with green onions then serve it warm.
5. Enjoy.

Full Vegetarian Stroganoff

🥣 Prep Time: 10 mins
🕒 Total Time: 30 mins

Servings per Recipe: 6
Calories   460.2
Fat   9.3g
Cholesterol   0.0mg
Sodium   517.4mg
Carbohydrates   79.2g
Protein   14.6g

Ingredients

- 1 (6 C.) packages pasta, egg-free ribbon noodles
- 1/4 C. margarine, vegan
- 1 onion, minced
- 16 oz. portabella mushrooms, sliced
- 2 garlic cloves, minced
- 2 C. vegetable broth, beef flavored
- 1 tsp salt
- 1 tsp black pepper
- 1 tbsp Worcestershire sauce, vegan
- 1/4 C. flour
- 1 C. vegan sour cream

Directions

1. Prepare the noodles by following the instructions on the package.
2. Place a pan over medium heat. Heat in it the margarine. Cook in it the onion with mushroom for 5 min.
3. Stir in the garlic and cook them for 1 min.
4. Place a saucepan over medium heat. Heat in it the broth until it starts boiling.
5. Stir in the salt, pepper and Worcestershire sauce. Add the flour and mix them well.
6. Let them cook until the sauce become thick. Add the sauce to the mushroom skillet.
7. Add the sour cream and stir them well. Serve your creamy mushroom right away with noodles.
8. Enjoy.

TUESDAY'S DINNER
Dinner (Herbed Mushroom Chicken with Rice)

Prep Time: 10 mins
Total Time: 1 hr 10 mins

Servings per Recipe: 4
Calories 779.0
Fat 34.0g
Cholesterol 137.3mg
Sodium 4189.8mg
Carbohydrates 80.8g
Protein 39.0g

Ingredients

1 tbsp olive oil
6 chicken thighs
1/2 tsp salt
1/2 tsp black pepper
2 tbsp butter
16 oz. button mushrooms, sliced
1 C. yellow onion, sliced
1 tbsp garlic, minced
2 tbsp all-purpose flour
2 tbsp tomato paste
2 C. dark chicken stock
2 tbsp rosemary leaves, chopped
4 C. steamed cooked white rice
2 tbsp parsley leaves, chopped
Country Spice Mix
2 1/2 tbsp paprika
2 tbsp salt
2 tbsp garlic powder
1 tbsp black pepper
1 tbsp onion powder
1 tbsp cayenne pepper
1 tbsp dried oregano
1 tbsp dried thyme

Directions

1. Rub the chicken thighs with the spice mix, some salt and pepper.
2. Place a skillet over medium heat. Heat in it the oil. Cook in it the chicken thighs for 4 to 5 min on each side.
3. Drain them and place them aside. Heat the butter in the same pan. Cook in it the mushroom for 5 min.
4. Stir in the onion with garlic. Cook them for 4 min. Add the flour and cook them for another 4 min while stirring them all the time.
5. Stir in the tomato paste with stock and rosemary. Let them cook until they start boiling.
6. Stir in the chicken back lower the heat. Let them cook for 35 min.
7. Once the time is up, flip the chicken thighs and cook them for an extra 35 min.
8. Serve your chicken and mushroom skillet warm with some rice.
9. Enjoy.

Parmesan Mushroom Breakfast

Prep Time: 5 mins
Total Time: 20 mins

Servings per Recipe: 2
Calories   478.7
Fat   33.5g
Cholesterol   610.5mg
Sodium   1309.7mg
Carbohydrates   12.1g
Protein   33.6g

Ingredients

- 2 tbsp butter
- 3 cloves garlic, minced
- 1/2 C. onion, sliced
- 8 oz. mushrooms, quartered
- 2 C. spinach, chopped
- 6 eggs
- 1/2 tsp salt
- 1 dash pepper
- 1/2 C. grated parmesan cheese

Directions

1. Before you do anything, preheat the oven broiler.
2. Place an ovenproof pan over medium heat. Heat in it the butter.
3. Cook in it the garlic with mushroom and onion for 5 min. Stir in the spinach and cook them for 3 min.
4. Get a mixing bowl: Whisk in it the eggs with a pinch of salt and pepper.
5. Add it to the mushroom mixture an swirl the pan to make it into an even layer.
6. Let it cook for 5 min over low heat until it starts to sit.
7. Top the mushroom tart with cheese. Place it in the oven and let it cook for 4 to 5 min.
8. Serve your breakfast mushroom tart warm.
9. Enjoy.

FLORIDA STYLE
Stuffed Mushroom with Shrimp Cream

Prep Time: 30 mins
Total Time: 45 mins

Servings per Recipe: 10
Calories	58.2
Fat	2.9g
Cholesterol	8.6mg
Sodium	95.2mg
Carbohydrates	3.7g
Protein	5.4g

Ingredients

- 40 medium mushroom caps, cleaned and drained
- 1/3 C. light cream cheese
- 1/4 C. low-fat milk
- 1 clove garlic, minced
- 1 pinch nutmeg
- 1 pinch pepper
- 1/2 tbsp flour
- 1 tbsp low-fat mayonnaise
- 1 tbsp lemon juice
- 3 tbsp parmesan cheese, Kraft
- 1 green onion, sliced thin
- 1 can crabmeat, drained
- 1 can baby shrimp, drained
- 1/2 C. light cheddar cheese, grated
- extra parmesan cheese

Directions

1. Before you do anything, preheat the oven to 400 F.
2. Place a saucepan over medium heat. Mix in it the flour, cream cheese, milk, garlic, salt, nutmeg, pepper and salt until they melt.
3. Mix in the mayonnaise, lemon juice, parmesan cheese and green onion.
4. Turn off the heat then stir in the shrimp with crab meat. Put on the lid and let the filling cool down completely.
5. Place the mushroom caps in a greased casserole dish. Spoon the filling into them.
6. Place the casserole in the oven and let it cook for 16 to 22 min. Serve it warm.
7. Enjoy.

Herbed Sautéed Mushroom Caps

Prep Time: 10 mins
Total Time: 15 mins

Servings per Recipe: 8
Calories   59.3
Fat   5.2g
Cholesterol   0.0mg
Sodium   149.5mg
Carbohydrates   2.2g
Protein   1.8g

Ingredients

- 1 lb. mushroom cap, stemmed and cleaned
- 3 tbsp olive oil
- 1/2 tsp salt
- 1/2 tsp paprika
- 1 garlic clove, crushed
- 1 green onion, chopped
- 3 tbsp fresh parsley, chopped
- 1 tbsp fresh dill weed, chopped
- 2 tsp basil

Directions

1. Place a pan over medium heat. Heat in it the oil. Cook in it the green onion with garlic, paprika and salt for 3 min.
2. Stir in the mushroom then cook for 6 min. Turn off the heat. Stir in the parsley with basil and dill.
3. Adjust the seasoning of your mushroom skillet then serve it warm with some sour cream.
4. Enjoy.

ASIAN-FUSION
Ginger Mushroom

Prep Time: 10 mins
Total Time: 35 mins

Servings per Recipe: 4
Calories   133.0
Fat   9.6g
Cholesterol   0.0mg
Sodium   512.9mg
Carbohydrates   8.4g
Protein   6.7g

Ingredients

2 tbsp peanut oil
1 1/2 lbs. white button mushrooms, cleaned quartered
1 tbsp sesame seeds, toasted
1 tbsp fresh ginger, minced
2 tbsp apple cider vinegar

1 tsp sugar
2 tbsp soy sauce
1 tsp toasted sesame oil
2 scallions, sliced

Directions

1. Place a pan over medium heat. Heat in it 1 tbsp of peanut oil. Cook in it the mushroom for 6 min.
2. Turn the heat to high and let it cook for 7 min. Stir in the remaining peanut oil.
3. Lower the heat and let them cook for an extra 8 min. Stir in the ginger with sesame seeds. Let them cook for 40 sec.
4. Stir in the rice vinegar, sugar and soy sauce. let them cook for 1 min while stirring them all the time.
5. Turn off the heat. Stir in the sesame oil. Garnish it with scallions then serve it warm with some sour cream.
6. Enjoy.

Full Fall Pot Roast

Prep Time: 20 mins
Total Time: 1 hr 35 mins

Servings per Recipe: 6
Calories 128.1
Fat 5.4g
Cholesterol 0.0mg
Sodium 119.0mg
Carbohydrates 17.7g
Protein 3.0g

Ingredients

- 3 - 4 lbs. pot roast, trimmed of fat
- flour
- 2 tbsp olive oil
- 2 C. sliced onions
- 1/4 C. water
- 1/4 C. ketchup
- 1/3 C. chicken broth
- 2 cloves garlic, minced
- 1/4 tsp dry mustard
- 1/4 tsp dried marjoram
- 1/4 tsp dried rosemary, crushed
- 1/4 tsp dried thyme
- 1 medium whole bay leaf
- 8 oz. mushrooms, whole
- 1/4 C. cold water
- 2 tbsp flour
- wide egg noodles, cooked and drained

Directions

1. Season the roast with some salt and pepper. Dust it with flour.
2. Place a large pot over medium heat. Heat in it 2 tbsp of olive oil.
3. Cook in it the roast for 2 to 3 min on each side.
4. Stir in the onion with 1/4 C. of water, 1/4 C. of ketchup, 1/3 C. broth, 1 large clove garlic, minced, 1/4 tsp each of dry mustard, marjoram, crushed rosemary, thyme and 1 medium whole bay leaf.
5. Bring them to a simmer. Lower the heat and put on the lid. Let them cook for 120 min over low heat.
6. Drain the roast and place it aside. Discard the bay leaf.
7. Get a small mixing bowl: Mix in it the cornstarch with 2 tbsp of flour.
8. Stir the mushroom into the pot with the cornstarch mix. Let them cook until the sauce becomes thick.
9. Adjust the seasoning of the sauce then spoon it over the roast. Serve it warm. Enjoy.

SAUCY
Red Button Skillet

🍳 Prep Time: 5 mins
⏱ Total Time: 25 mins

Servings per Recipe: 6
Calories 32.0
Fat 2.3g
Cholesterol 0.0mg
Sodium 0.9mg
Carbohydrates 2.8g
Protein 0.3g

Ingredients

1 tbsp oil
1 large onion, chopped
1 can button mushroom, rinsed
1 tbsp any soup mix
1 tsp paprika
1/2 tsp black pepper, grated
water

Directions

1. Place a skillet over medium heat. Heat in it the oil. Cook in it the onion for 5 min.
2. Stir in the mushroom and let them cook for an extra 6 min.
3. Stir in the soup mix with paprika, a pinch of salt and pepper. Cook them for 1 min.
4. Stir a splash of water to make the sauce a bit thin. Let them cook until it becomes thick to your liking.
5. Serve your cream mushroom warm with some rice, noodles or leftover meat.
6. Enjoy.

Roasted Honey Mushroom Chicken

Prep Time: 10 mins
Total Time: 1 hr 10 mins

Servings per Recipe: 4
Calories   421.3
Fat   24.1g
Cholesterol   92.8mg
Sodium   685.0mg
Carbohydrates   18.0g
Protein   33.6g

Ingredients

4 chicken breasts
1 medium red bell pepper, cored, seeded and strips
1 medium yellow bell pepper
1/2 lb. mushroom, cleaned and quartered
1 (14 oz.) cans diced tomatoes, drained
3 tbsp olive oil
2 tbsp balsamic vinegar
1 tbsp rosemary
1 tsp salt
ground black pepper
salt
1 1/2 tbsp honey

Directions

1. Before you do anything, preheat the oven to 425 F.
2. Get a baking dish. Combine in it the mushroom with tomato, bell peppers, olive oil, vinegar, rosemary, salt and pepper.
3. Add the chicken breasts on top and press them into the mix. Sprinkle over them some salt and pepper followed by the honey.
4. Place the dish in the oven and let it cook for 1 h.
5. Serve your chicken and mushroom casserole warm with some rice.
6. Enjoy.

CALIFORNIA
Pizza Pan

🥣 Prep Time: 10 mins
⏱ Total Time: 45 mins

Servings per Recipe: 4
Calories   260.7
Fat   18.1g
Cholesterol   53.5mg
Sodium   678.9mg
Carbohydrates   14.9g
Protein   11.3g

Ingredients

1 1/2 tbsp olive oil
2 large onions, sliced
2 tsp honey
2 tsp balsamic vinegar
8 oz. fresh mushrooms, sliced
12 inches pizza crusts
8 oz. crumbled feta cheese
1 tsp dried thyme

Directions

1. Before you do anything, preheat the oven to 450 F.
2. Place a pan over medium heat. Heat in it the oil. Cook in it the onion for 11 min.
3. Stir in the vinegar with honey. Cook them for 9 min. Stir in a pinch of salt and pepper to make the sauce.
4. Lay the pizza crust on a baking sheet. Top it with mushroom, cheese, thyme, a pinch of salt and pepper.
5. Place the pizza in the oven and let it cook for 16 min. Serve it warm.
6. Enjoy.

Grated Spud and Mushroom Frittata

Prep Time: 5 mins
Total Time: 15 mins

Servings per Recipe: 1
Calories   409.3
Fat   19.2g
Cholesterol   401.6mg
Sodium   333.3mg
Carbohydrates   35.1g
Protein   24.5g

Ingredients

- 2 large eggs
- 1 small potato, grated
- 1/4 C. cheddar cheese, grated
- 1 tsp dried chives
- 1 small tomatoes, diced
- 1 large mushroom, diced
- ground black pepper

Directions

1. Before you do anything, preheat the oven to 350 F.
2. Get a mixing bowl: Mix in it the eggs. Add the cheese with chives and potato. Combine them well.
3. Place a pan over low medium heat. Coat it with oil and heat. Pour in it the eggs mixture.
4. Lay over it the mushroom and tomato slices. Sprinkle over them some salt and pepper.
5. Let it cook for 12 to 16 min. Serve it warm.
6. Enjoy.

THURSDAY MORNING
Omelet

Prep Time: 10 mins
Total Time: 20 mins

Servings per Recipe: 2
Calories 415.2
Fat 35.5g
Cholesterol 452.2mg
Sodium 291.1mg
Carbohydrates 4.9g
Protein 20.0g

Ingredients

4 large eggs, beaten
1/4 C. cream
2 tbsp butter
1/4 lb. mushroom, sliced
1/2 garlic clove, crushed
1 pinch red pepper flakes
1/4 tsp thyme leave
1 tbsp sliced chives
1/3 C. Swiss cheese, shredded

Directions

1. Get a mixing bowl: Whisk in it the eggs with cream.
2. Place a pan over medium heat. Heat in it 1 tbsp of butter. Cook in it the mushroom with butter for 6 min.
3. Stir in the thyme with pepper flakes and chives. Cook them for 30 sec. Pour in the egg mix.
4. Stir them while cooking until they start to sit. Add the cheese and sit them until they are done.
5. Serve your mushroom omelet warm.
6. Enjoy.

Tortellini Soup Toscano

> 🥣 Prep Time: 15 mins
> 🕐 Total Time: 45 mins
>
> Servings per Recipe: 4
> Calories   456.2
> Fat   17.5g
> Cholesterol   94.5mg
> Sodium   633.8mg
> Carbohydrates   41.0g
> Protein   36.1g

Ingredients

2 tbsp butter
1/4 C. carrot, chopped
1 stalk celery, chopped
1 medium onion, chopped
1 tbsp garlic, minced
1/2 tsp thyme, minced
1 tsp Mrs. Dash seasoning mix
8 oz. sliced mushrooms

6 C. low sodium chicken broth
9 oz. 3 cheese tortellini
2 C. cooked chicken, chopped
2 C. baby spinach leaves, loosely packed
parmesan cheese, grated

Directions

1. Place a large pot over medium heat. Melt in it the butter.
2. Cook in it the carrots, celery, onions, and garlic for 9 min.
3. Stir in the mushrooms, fresh thyme, and Mrs. Dash. Cook them for 7 min.
4. Stir in the broth and bring them to a boil. Stir in the tortellini with chicken.
5. Let them cook for 8 to 10 min. Stir in the spinach and let them cook for an extra 6 min.
6. Adjust the seasoning of your soup then serve it hot.
7. Enjoy.

HERBED
Mushroom Cakes

Prep Time: 15 mins
Total Time: 31 mins

Servings per Recipe: 8
Calories   138.3
Fat   7.4g
Cholesterol   69.8mg
Sodium   161.3mg
Carbohydrates   12.8g
Protein   5.1g

Ingredients

3 slightly beaten eggs
3 C. mushrooms, chopped
1/2 C. all-purpose flour
1/2 C. seasoned dry breadcrumb
1/3 C. onion, chopped
1 medium jalapeno pepper, chopped

1/4 C. parsley, chopped
1/4 tsp pepper
3 tbsp vegetable oil

Directions

1. Before you do anything, preheat the oven to 350 F.
2. Get a mixing bowl: Mix in the eggs, mushrooms, flour, bread crumbs, onion, jalapeño, parsley and pepper.
3. Place a pan over medium heat. Heat in it the oil.
4. Form 1/4 C. of the mushroom mixture into a cake and place it in the hot pan.
5. Repeat the process with the remaining mixture. Cook them for 3 to 5 min on each side.
6. Drain the mushroom cakes and repeat the process with the remaining mixture.
7. Serve your mushroom cakes with your favorite toppings.
8. Enjoy.

Steak and Potato Dump Dinner with Gravy

Prep Time: 10 mins
Total Time: 7 hrs 10 mins

Servings per Recipe: 6
Calories 69.7
Fat 3.1g
Cholesterol 0.0mg
Sodium 906.0mg
Carbohydrates 8.8g
Protein 1.9g

Ingredients

2 - 2 1/2 lbs. boneless round steak, cut into 6 pieces
1 1/4 oz. dry onion soup mix
10 3/4 oz. condensed cream of mushroom soup, undiluted
1/2 C. beef broth
1 C. mushroom, sliced
1/2 C. onion, chopped
mashed potatoes

Directions

1. Stir all the ingredients in a slow cooker.
2. Put on the lid and let them cook for 8 h on low.
3. Once the time is up, serve your steak and mushroom gravy warm with some rice or noodles.
4. Enjoy.

BAJA Mushroom Quesadillas

Prep Time: 25 mins
Total Time: 31 mins

Servings per Recipe: 1
Calories   378.6
Fat   23.4g
Cholesterol   86.0mg
Sodium   370.8mg
Carbohydrates   20.3g
Protein   22.9g

Ingredients

- 1/4-1/3 C. butter
- 2 -3 tsp chili powder
- 1 tbsp minced garlic
- 1 tsp dried oregano
- 10 oz. white button mushrooms, sliced
- 2 C. cooked chicken, chopped
- 1/2 C. onion, chopped
- 1/4 C. cilantro
- 3 C. cheddar cheese
- 16 corn tortillas
- olive oil
- salt and black pepper
- salsa

Directions

1. Place a pan over medium heat. Heat in it the butter. Cook in it the chili powder, garlic and oregano for 40 sec.
2. Stir in the mushroom. Cook them for 11 min. Stir in the chicken, onion and cilantro.
3. Sprinkle over them some salt and pepper. Turn off the heat and let them sit for 22 min.
4. Before you do anything, preheat the grill and grease it.
5. Coat one side of 8 tortillas with oil. Lay them on a baking pan with the greased side facing down.
6. Spoon into the mushroom and chicken mix. Cover them with the remaining 8 tortillas.
7. Grease their top with oil and place them on the grill. Let them cook for 3 to 4 min on each side.
8. Slice the tortillas into wedges then serve them hot with some sour cream.
9. Enjoy.

Creamy Weekend Fettuccine

Prep Time: 10 mins
Total Time: 25 mins

Servings per Recipe: 4
Calories   720.0
Fat   42.2g
Cholesterol   210.2mg
Sodium   377.4mg
Carbohydrates   70.2g
Protein   17.6g

Ingredients

6 tbsp butter
1 small onion, chopped
4 garlic cloves, minced
12 oz. mushrooms, chopped
salt and pepper
1 C. heavy cream
2 tbsp chopped thyme
2 tbsp lemon juice

2 tsp soy sauce
1 lb. cooked fettuccine pasta
parmesan cheese

Directions

1. Prepare the pasta by following the instructions on the package.
2. Place a pan over medium heat. Heat in it the butter.
3. Sauté in it the garlic with onion, a pinch of salt and pepper for 4 min.
4. Stir in the mushroom and let them cook for 4 min.
5. Stir in the thyme with cream. Bring them to a rolling boil for 4 to 5 min.
6. Add the lemon juice with soy sauce. Turn off the heat.
7. Add the mushroom sauce to the noodles and toss it to coat. Serve it warm.
8. Enjoy.

BAKED Rice

Prep Time: 20 mins
Total Time: 1 hr 10 mins

Servings per Recipe: 6
Calories 205.7
Fat 8.3g
Cholesterol 20.3mg
Sodium 639.2mg
Carbohydrates 27.2g
Protein 5.0g

Ingredients

1 C. uncooked long grain rice
1/4 C. butter
1/2 C. chopped celery
1/2 C. chopped onion
1 C. sliced fresh mushrooms
1 (14 1/2 oz.) cans chicken broth

1/3 C. water
2 tbsp soy sauce
1 tbsp parsley flakes

Directions

1. Before you do anything, preheat the oven to 350 F.
2. Place a pan over medium heat. Stir in it the butter with rice. Cook them for 3 min.
3. Stir in the onion with celery. Let them cook for 3 min.
4. Stir in the mushroom and cook them for 5 min. Spoon the mixture into a greased casserole dish.
5. Add to it the broth with parsley, soy sauce, water, a pinch of salt and pepper. Stir them well.
6. Place the pan in the oven and let it cook for 46 to 52 min. Serve it hot.
7. Enjoy

Pennsylvania Inspired Cabbage Skillet

 Prep Time: 10 mins
 Total Time: 18 mins

Servings per Recipe: 4
Calories   152.3
Fat   12.3g
Cholesterol   32.0mg
Sodium   135.2mg
Carbohydrates   9.8g
Protein   3.1g

Ingredients

- 2 oz. butter
- 4 slices turkey bacon, chopped
- 8 mushrooms, sliced
- 22 oz. cabbage, shredded
- 1 spring onion
- black pepper

Directions

1. Place a skillet over medium heat. Heat in it the butter.
2. Cook in it the bacon with mushroom for 2 min. Stir in the cabbage and let them cook for 6 min.
3. Add the spring onion with a pinch of salt and pepper. Serve it warm.
4. Enjoy.

BROOKE'S
Burgers

Prep Time: 5 mins
Total Time: 17 mins

Servings per Recipe: 1
Calories 547.7
Fat 29.5g
Cholesterol 110.9mg
Sodium 1794.1mg
Carbohydrates 30.8g
Protein 40.0g

Ingredients

1 tsp extra virgin olive oil
2 oz. mushrooms, chopped
1 small garlic clove, sliced
1/8 tsp kosher salt
4 oz. lean ground sirloin
1 scallion, chopped
1 tbsp soy sauce
1/4 tsp ground black pepper

1 slice Swiss cheese
1 seeded hamburger bun, toasted
1 tbsp Dijon mustard
2 small romaine lettuce leaves
2 slices tomatoes

Directions

1. Before you do anything, preheat the oven broiler. Place the rack 6 inches away from the heat.
2. Place a pan over medium heat. Heat in it the oil. Cook in it the mushrooms, garlic and salt for 6 min.
3. Turn off the heat and let them cool down for a while.
4. Get a mixing bowl: Toss in it the sirloin, scallion, soy sauce, pepper and cooled mushrooms and mix.
5. Shape the mixture into burger. Place it on a baking sheet and cook it in the oven for 4 min on each side.
6. Serve your burgers with your favorite toppings.
7. Enjoy.

Mushroom Loaves

Prep Time: 15 mins
Total Time: 55 mins

Servings per Recipe: 8
Calories   298.2
Fat   15.5g
Cholesterol   41.3mg
Sodium   361.4mg
Carbohydrates   27.5g
Protein   11.9g

Ingredients

- 1 loaf round unsliced bread
- 8 oz. Swiss cheese
- 1 C. mushrooms, sliced
- 1/4 C. butter
- 1 1/2 tsp poppy seeds
- 2 garlic cloves
- 1/2 tsp seasoning salt
- 1/2 tsp ground mustard
- 1/2 tsp lemon juice

Directions

1. Before you do anything, preheat the oven to 350 F.
2. Use a sharp knife to cut the bread into 1/4 inch thick slits leaving about 1 inch of the base intact.
3. Slice the Swiss cheese into 1/2 inch dices. Place the cheese and mushroom slices into the bread pockets.
4. Place the stuffed bread on a baking sheet and place it aside.
5. Get a microwave safe bowl: Mix in it the butter, poppy seeds, minced garlic, seasoned salt, ground mustard, and lemon juice.
6. Place it in the microwave and cover it. Cook it for 2 min.
7. Drizzle the mixture over the stuffed bread. Place it in the oven and cover it with a piece of foil.
8. Let it cook for 42 min then serve it warm.
9. Enjoy.

MAYLENE'S Stuffed Mushrooms

🥣 Prep Time: 20 mins
⏱ Total Time: 35 mins

Servings per Recipe: 6
Calories 277.9
Fat 15.0g
Cholesterol 86.1mg
Sodium 832.4mg
Carbohydrates 14.9g
Protein 21.1g

Ingredients

1 lb. mushrooms, cleaned
1/4 C. celery, chopped
2 tbsp onions, chopped
2 tbsp red bell peppers, chopped
1/2 lb. crabmeat
2 C. oyster crackers, crushed
1/2 C. cheddar cheese, shredded
1/4 tsp garlic powder

1/2 tsp Old Bay Seasoning
1/4 tsp black pepper, ground
1/4 tsp salt
1 egg
1/2 C. water
6 slices white cheddar cheese

Directions

1. Before you do anything, preheat the oven to 400 F.
2. Slice off the stems of the mushrooms. Chop half of the mushroom stems.
3. Place a pan over medium heat. Heat in it the butter.
4. Cook in it the chopped stems with, celery, onion and pepper for 3 min.
5. Turn off the heat and let the mixture cool down completely.
6. Get a mixing bowl: Combine in it the mushroom mixture with bell peppers, crabmeat, garlic powder, old bay seasoning, water, egg, cheddar cheese and a pinch of salt.
7. Place the mushroom caps in a greased casserole dish. Spoon into it the filling.
8. Top them with the white cheddar slices. Place the casserole in the oven and let them cook for 14 to 16 min.
9. Serve your stuffed mushroom casserole warm.
10. Enjoy.

Potato Pierogis with Saucy Mushrooms

Prep Time: 5 mins
Total Time: 15 mins

Servings per Recipe: 4
Calories   71.3
Fat   2.5g
Cholesterol   4.5mg
Sodium   72.9mg
Carbohydrates   8.0g
Protein   3.5g

Ingredients

- 1 tsp olive oil
- 2 C. sliced mushrooms
- 1 onion, sliced
- salt and pepper
- 2 tbsp apple cider vinegar
- 1 tbsp flour
- 2/3 C. low-fat milk
- 1/4 C. chicken broth
- 1 (1 lb.) package frozen low-fat potato pierogis, thawed
- 2 tbsp light sour cream

Directions

1. Place a pan over medium heat. Heat in it the oil. Cook in it the mushroom with onion, a pinch of salt and pepper for 5 min.
2. Add the apple cider vinegar and cook them for 2 min. Add the flour and mix them well.
3. Add the milk with broth, and pierogis. Let them cook until they start boiling.
4. Turn off the heat and add the sour cream. Adjust the seasoning of your soup then serve it hot.
5. Enjoy.

HEIRLOOM
Crepes

🥣 Prep Time: 20 mins
🕒 Total Time: 48 mins

Servings per Recipe: 4
Calories   439.0
Fat   34.0g
Cholesterol   72.2mg
Sodium   605.2mg
Carbohydrates   10.2g
Protein   26.9g

Ingredients

12 (6 inch) crepes
3 tbsp extra virgin olive oil
1 1/4 lbs. mushrooms, rinsed, trimmed and sliced
1/4 C. flat-leaf parsley, chopped
1 tbsp thyme leave
1 garlic clove, chopped
salt & pepper

1 (10 oz.) packages spinach, washed, stemmed & chopped
5 oz. goat cheese, crumbled
2 C. mozzarella cheese, shredded

Directions

1. Before you do anything, preheat the oven to 350 F.
2. Place a pan over medium heat. Heat in it the oil. Cook in it the mushroom with a pinch of salt for 11 min.
3. Add the parsley, thyme, garlic, salt and pepper. Let them cook for 2 min.
4. Lower the heat and add the spinach. Put on the lid and let them cook for 3 min.
5. Stir in the goat cheese until it melts to make the filling.
6. Lay a crepe on a chopping board. Place in it some of the filling then roll it.
7. Repeat the process with the remaining filling and crepes. Place them in a greased casserole dish.
8. Lay a piece of foil over it to cover it. Cook it in the oven for 16 min.
9. Serve them warm with some sour cream.
10. Enjoy.

Handmade Cheese Raviolis

Prep Time: 1 hr 30 mins
Total Time: 1 hr 40 mins

Servings per Recipe: 4
Calories   651.1
Fat   28.0g
Cholesterol   160.3mg
Sodium   679.7mg
Carbohydrates   75.4g
Protein   23.0g

Ingredients

Insides
1/4 C. sliced shiitake mushroom
1/4 C. sliced oyster mushroom
1/2 C. sliced cremini mushroom
1/2 C. sliced white button mushrooms
2 garlic cloves, sliced
1/4 C. butter
1/4 tsp ground black pepper
1/8 tsp sea salt
1/4 tsp onion powder
1/4 tsp garlic powder
1/8 C. beef broth

1 tbsp olive oil
1 C. ricotta cheese
1/4 C. parmesan cheese, grated
1/2 C. of chopped mixed mushrooms
Raviolis
3 C. unbleached white flour
1/2 tsp salt
2 eggs
1/2 C. water

Directions

1. To make the filling:
2. Place a pan over medium heat. Heat in it the butter. Cook in it the mushrooms for 5 min.
3. Stir in the pepper, salt, and onion/garlic powder. Stir in 1/8 C. of beef broth. Let them cook for 3 min.
4. Turn off the heat and let it cool down for a while. Stir in the cheeses.
5. To make the dough:
6. Get a mixing bowl: Stir in the salt with flour. Add the eggs and mix them well.
7. Knead the dough with your hands until it becomes soft. Place it in a greased bowl and cover it with a cling wrap
8. Let the dough rest for 16 min.
9. Slice the dough in half. Place a half on a floured board. Roll it until it becomes 1/8 inches thick.

10. Cut the dough into squares and place them on a lined up baking sheet. Place about 1 tsp of the filling in middle of each square.
11. Repeat the process with the other half of dough. Use them to cover the squares with the filling.
12. Press the edges to seal them with your fingers or a fork. Let them dry for 60 min.
13. Once the time is up, bring 7 quarts of water in a large pot to a boil with some salt.
14. Lower in it the ravioli squares and cook them for 11 to 16 min until they rise on top.
15. Drain the raviolis and place them on a serving plate.
16. Toss them with some butter and serve them with your favorite sauce.
17. Enjoy.

Mushroom Stir Fry 101

Prep Time: 5 mins
Total Time: 15 mins

Servings per Recipe: 6
Calories   40.8
Fat   1.8g
Cholesterol   0.0mg
Sodium   21.4mg
Carbohydrates   5.1g
Protein   2.5g

Ingredients

- 2 tsp olive oil
- 2 - 3 cloves garlic, minced
- 2 C. sliced button mushrooms
- 4 C. chopped broccoli
- 1 tbsp chopped rosemary
- salt & ground black pepper

Directions

1. Place a pan over medium heat. Heat in it the oil. Cook in it the garlic for 40 sec.
2. Stir in the mushroom and cook them for 4 min.
3. Stir in the rosemary with broccoli, a pinch of salt and pepper. Cook them for 4 min.
4. Serve your salad warm.
5. Enjoy.

GARLICKY
Mushroom Skillet with Peas

Prep Time: 5 mins
Total Time: 20 mins

Servings per Recipe: 4
Calories   203.8
Fat   12.1g
Cholesterol   30.5mg
Sodium   226.9mg
Carbohydrates   17.8g
Protein   7.8g

Ingredients

1 (16 oz.) bags frozen peas
8 oz. sliced mushrooms
2 - 4 garlic cloves
4 tbsp butter

salt and pepper

Directions

1. Place a pan over medium heat. Heat in it the butter. Cook in it the garlic with mushroom for 6 min.
2. Stir in the peas and cook them for 2 min.
3. Put on the lid and let them cook for 16 min.
4. Serve your mushroom skillet warm.
5. Enjoy.

How to Make Orzo

Prep Time: 5 mins
Total Time: 30 mins

Servings per Recipe: 3
Calories	486.1
Fat	26.2g
Cholesterol	73.8mg
Sodium	402.3mg
Carbohydrates	44.8g
Protein	17.6g

Ingredients

- 1 C. uncooked orzo pasta
- 1 C. shredded Swiss cheese
- 4 tbsp butter, divided
- 2 tsp minced garlic
- 1/4 tsp salt
- 1/4 tsp pepper
- 1/2 C. sliced mushrooms

Directions

1. Prepare the orzo by following the instructions on the package.
2. Melt 3 tbsp of butter. Toss it with cheese, garlic, salt and pepper in a large mixing bowl.
3. Place a saucepan over medium heat. Heat in it the rest of the butter.
4. Cook in it the mushrooms for 5 min. Stir in the orzo, cheese mixture, a pinch of salt and pepper.
5. Heat them until the cheese melts. Serve it warm.
6. Enjoy.

FRIDAY NIGHT
Linguine

Prep Time: 5 mins
Total Time: 15 mins

Servings per Recipe: 4
Calories   611.8
Fat   37.8g
Cholesterol   210.1mg
Sodium   402.0mg
Carbohydrates   45.7g
Protein   23.1g

Ingredients

1 (8 oz.) packages linguine
2 tbsp butter
1/2 lb. mushrooms, sliced
1/2 C. butter
2 garlic cloves, minced
1 (3 oz.) packages cream cheese
2 tbsp parsley, chopped
3/4 tsp dried basil

2/3 C. boiling water
1/2 lb. cooked shrimp

Directions

1. Prepare the pasta by following the instructions on the package. Drain it and place it aside.
2. Place a pan over medium heat. Heat in it 2 tbsp of butter. Cook in it the mushrooms for 6 min.
3. Drain it and place it aside. Heat 1/2 C. of butter in the same pan. Cook in it the garlic for 40 sec.
4. Add the cream cheese and stir it until it melts. Add the basil with parsley.
5. Let them cook for 6 min. Add the boiling water and stir them well. Stir in the shrimp with mushroom.
6. Let them cook for 3 min. Stir in the pasta with a pinch of salt and pepper. Serve your creamy pasta warm.
7. Enjoy.

Broiled Halibut with Mushroom Salsa

Prep Time: 10 mins
Total Time: 20 mins

Servings per Recipe: 4
Calories   452.2
Fat   12.0g
Cholesterol   206.9mg
Sodium   587.0mg
Carbohydrates   4.6g
Protein   77.1g

Ingredients

2 C. sliced cremini mushrooms
2 green onions, sliced
1/3 C. light mayonnaise
2 tbsp parsley, chopped
1 tbsp lemon juice
1 tsp gingerroot, grated
1/4 tsp salt
1/4 tsp pepper
4 halibut steaks

Directions

1. Before you do anything, preheat the oven broiler.
2. Get a mixing bowl: Toss in it the mushrooms, onions, mayonnaise, parsley, lemon juice, ginger, salt and pepper.
3. Lay the fish on a greased baking pan. Place it in the oven and cook it for 6 min.
4. Flip the fish gently then top it with the mushroom mixture.
5. Place it in the oven broiler and let it cook until the fish is done for about 8 to 12 min.
6. Enjoy.

ONTARIO
Casserole

Prep Time: 20 mins
Total Time: 1 hr 30 mins

Servings per Recipe: 8
Calories   254.0
Fat   13.4g
Cholesterol   15.4mg
Sodium   323.3mg
Carbohydrates 29.8g
Protein   5.1g

Ingredients

- 1/2 C. wild rice
- 1/2 C. pearl barley
- 1/2 C. brown rice
- 1/4 C. oil
- 1 large onion, sliced
- 4 garlic cloves, chopped
- 4 tbsp butter
- 1/2 lb. mushroom, sliced
- 3 1/2 C. broth
- 1 tsp crushed dried thyme
- 1/2 tsp crushed dried oregano
- salt & pepper

Directions

1. Before you do anything, preheat the oven to 350 F.
2. Get a mixing bowl: Stir in the wild and brown rice with barley.
3. Place an ovenproof pot over medium heat. Heat in it the oil. Cook in it the garlic with onion for 6 min.
4. Stir in the rice and barley mix. Cook them for 2 min.
5. Place a small skillet over medium heat. Heat in it the butter. Cook in it the mushroom for 2 min.
6. Add it to the saucepan with broth, herbs, a pinch of salt and pepper. Cook them until they start boiling.
7. Put on the lid and place the pot in the oven for 60 min. Serve it hot.
8. Enjoy.

Extra Cheesy Mushroom Pizza

Prep Time: 10 mins
Total Time: 40 mins

Servings per Recipe: 4
Calories   490.5
Fat   38.0g
Cholesterol   93.9mg
Sodium   461.4mg
Carbohydrates   9.1g
Protein   29.6g

Ingredients

- 14 oz. refrigerated prepared pizza crust
- 3 tbsp extra virgin olive oil
- 3 garlic cloves, chopped
- 5 oz. shiitake mushrooms, stems discarded and sliced
- 8 oz. white mushrooms, sliced
- salt
- 2 C. Swiss cheese, shredded
- 2 C. mozzarella cheese, shredded

Directions

1. Before you do anything, preheat the oven to 400 F.
2. Lay the pizza dough on a baking pan. Coat it with 2 tbsp of olive oil. Sprinkle over it the garlic.
3. Place the pizza crust in the oven and let it cook for 9 min.
4. Place a pan over medium heat. Heat in it the remaining oil. Cook in it the remaining mushroom for 9 min.
5. Top the pizza crust with Swiss cheese, cooked mushroom then mozzarella cheese on top.
6. Place the pizza in the oven and let it cook for 16 min. Serve it warm.
7. Enjoy.

SIMPLE
Miso Soup

Prep Time: 5 mins
Total Time: 15 mins

Servings per Recipe: 1
Calories   70.4
Fat   2.3g
Cholesterol   0.0mg
Sodium   631.4mg
Carbohydrates   8.5g
Protein   5.3g

Ingredients

1/2 pint water
2 shiitake mushrooms, sliced
1 scallion, white part sliced
1 tbsp miso

1 oz. firm tofu, diced

Directions

1. Place a saucepan over medium heat. Heat in it the water until it starts boiling.
2. Add to it the miso with mushroom. Lower the heat and let them cook for 6 min.
3. Pour the soup into serving bowls. Stir into it the scallions and tofu.
4. Serve your soup right away.
5. Enjoy.

Maria's Quesadilla

Prep Time: 15 mins
Total Time: 25 mins

Servings per Recipe: 1
Calories   783.1
Fat   36.9g
Cholesterol   59.3mg
Sodium   1251.5mg
Carbohydrates   84.2g
Protein   29.0g

Ingredients

1 medium red onion, chopped
1/2 lb. mushrooms, diced
1 clove garlic, minced
1 tsp oregano
2 tbsp olive oil

2 tomatoes, deseeded &,chopped
2 C. red peppers, diced
8 tortillas
2 C. grated cheddar cheese

Directions

1. Before you do anything, preheat the oven to 350 F.
2. Place a pan over medium heat. Heat in it the oil. Cook in it the onion with garlic, oregano, mushroom, a pinch of salt and pepper.
3. Let them cook for 6 min. Add the tomato an cook them for an extra 6 min.
4. Lay 4 tortillas in the bottom of a greased baking pan. Pour over it the mushroom mixture.
5. Sprinkle the cheese on top then cover them with the rest of the tortillas.
6. Place the tortilla casserole in the oven. Let it cook for 11 min. Serve it hot with some sour cream.
7. Enjoy.

VEAL CUTS with Mushroom Sauce

Prep Time: 10 mins
Total Time: 30 mins

Servings per Recipe: 4
Calories   150.0
Fat   10.4g
Cholesterol   12.0mg
Sodium   96.4mg
Carbohydrates   10.8g
Protein   5.1g

Ingredients

4 veal chops
2 tbsp olive oil
salt and pepper
1 tbsp tarragon
1 lb. cremini mushroom, sliced
2 tbsp flour
1 C. chicken stock
2 tbsp heavy cream
1 dash nutmeg

Directions

1. Season the veal chops with some salt and pepper.
2. Place a pan over medium heat. Heat in it the oil. Cook in it the veal chops for 6 min on each sides.
3. Drain them and place them aside.
4. Get a mixing bowl: Stir in the mushroom with flour, a pinch of salt and pepper.
5. Stir them into the pan and let them cook for 4 min.
6. Stir in the stock and cook for 5 min until it becomes thick. Stir in the cream with nutmeg, a pinch of salt and pepper.
7. Place the veal chops on serving plates. Spoon the mushroom sauce over them.
8. Serve it warm.
9. Enjoy.

Mushroom Pesto Spaghetti

Prep Time: 10 mins
Total Time: 20 mins

Servings per Recipe: 4
Calories   244.0
Fat   4.7g
Cholesterol   0.0mg
Sodium   8.6mg
Carbohydrates   38.6g
Protein   12.1g

Ingredients

7 oz. thin spaghetti
1 - 2 tbsp olive oil
1/2 onion, slivered
1 red bell pepper, cored and slivered
8 oz. mushrooms, sliced

7 oz. pesto sauce

Directions

1. Prepare the pasta by following the instructions on the package.
2. Place a pan over medium heat. Heat in it the oil. Cook in it the onion for 4 min.
3. Stir in the peppers with mushroom. Cook them for 5 min. Stir in the pesto with spaghetti, a pinch of salt and pepper.
4. Serve it warm with some bread sticks.
5. Enjoy.

CLASSIC
Turkey and Parsley Sauce

🥣 Prep Time: 15 mins
⏲ Total Time: 50 mins

Servings per Recipe: 4
Calories 96.7
Fat 6.7g
Cholesterol 7.8mg
Sodium 534.4mg
Carbohydrates 7.2g
Protein 3.0g

Ingredients

9 oz. button mushrooms, sliced
4 turkey fillets
3 tbsp flour
1 garlic clove, diced
1 tbsp butter
1 tbsp olive oil
1 tbsp chicken bouillon powder

1 tsp parsley, minced
1/4 tsp salt
1 C. warm water

Directions

1. Before you do anything, preheat the oven to 350 F.
2. Get a shallow bowl: Stir in the garlic with flour and salt.
3. Dust the turkey fillets with the flour mixture.
4. Place a pan over medium heat. Heat in it the butter. Cook in it the turkey fillets for 10 to 12 min on each side
5. Drain them and place them on serving plate.
6. Heat the oil in the same pan. Cook in it the mushroom for 11 min.
7. Get a mixing bowl: Stir in the bouillon powder with water and parsley. Stir it into the mushroom pan.
8. Let them cook for 4 to 6 min until the sauce becomes thick.
9. Spoon the hot sauce over the turkey fillets. Serve them warm with some rice.
10. Enjoy.

Balsamic Mushroom Buttons

Prep Time: 5 mins
Total Time: 35 mins

Servings per Recipe: 4
Calories	66.9
Fat	3.6g
Cholesterol	0.0mg
Sodium	5.0mg
Carbohydrates	7.7g
Protein	2.4g

Ingredients

- 1 tbsp olive oil
- 1 sprig rosemary, minced
- 1 garlic clove, minced
- 1 tbsp honey
- 1 tbsp balsamic vinegar
- salt and pepper
- 10 oz. fresh button mushrooms

Directions

1. Before you do anything, preheat the oven to 325 F.
2. Place a pan over medium heat. Stir in it the oil with rosemary, garlic and honey for 2 min.
3. Stir in the mushroom with balsamic vinegar. Spoon the mixture into a greased baking dish.
4. Place it in the oven and let it cook for 35 to 42 min. Serve your sweet mushroom warm as a topping or side dish.
5. Enjoy.

TRUE Country Pilaf

Prep Time: 10 mins
Total Time: 1 hr 10 mins

Servings per Recipe: 1
Calories	100.3
Fat	1.8g
Cholesterol	0.0mg
Sodium	70.4mg
Carbohydrates	18.3g
Protein	3.7g

Ingredients

- 1 tbsp vegetable oil
- 8 oz. portabella mushrooms, chopped
- 1 small onion, chopped
- 2 garlic cloves, minced
- 1 1/4 C. pearl barley, uncooked
- 3 C. fat-free low-sodium chicken broth
- 1/4 tsp salt
- 1/4 tsp pepper
- 2 tbsp dill weed, snipped

Directions

1. Place a saucepan over medium heat. Heat in it the oil. Cook in it the mushrooms with onion and garlic for 6 min.
2. Add the barley and cook them for 2 min. Add the broth with a pinch of salt and pepper. Cook them until they start boiling over high heat.
3. Lower the heat and put on the lid. Let them cook for 46 to 52 min until the barley is done. Serve it hot.
4. Enjoy.

Mushroom Wellington

Prep Time: 30 mins
Total Time: 1 hr

Servings per Recipe: 6
Calories 907.6
Fat 59.8g
Cholesterol 147.7mg
Sodium 589.3mg
Carbohydrates 44.0g
Protein 31.2g

Ingredients

- 2 tbsp butter
- 3 shallots, chopped
- 1 C. wild mushroom
- 2 oz. grape juice
- 2 oz. heavy cream
- 4 beef tenderloin steaks
- olive oil flavored cooking spray
- 3 shallots, chopped
- 2 C. vegetable broth
- 2 C. chicken broth
- 1 tsp cornstarch
- 2 sheets puff pastry
- 1 egg
- 1 pinch salt
- 1 pinch pepper

Directions

1. To make the filling:
2. Place a pan over medium heat. Heat in it the butter. Cook in it the shallots for 3 min.
3. Stir in the mushroom and cook them for 4 min. Stir in the grape juice then let them cook for another 3 min.
4. Stir in the cream and let them cook for 2 to 3 min. Pour the mixture into a food blender. Blend it smooth.
5. Pour the filling into a mixing bowl. Season it with some salt and pepper.
6. Sprinkle some salt and pepper all over the steaks.
7. Place a large skillet over medium heat. Grease it with a cooking spray. Cook in it the steaks for 4 to 5 min on each side.
8. Before you do anything, preheat the oven to 425 F.
9. Place the steaks in a roasting pan. Cook them in the oven until they reach 100 f internal temperature.
10. Once the time is up, place the steaks on a large plate and let them cool down completely.

Reserve the steaks drippings.
11. Preheat the oven to 400 F.
12. Cut the pastry into 4 pieces. Lay each steak on a pastry sheet. Spread over it the mushroom mixture.
13. Pull the dough over the steak with filling and press the edges to seal them. Repeat the process with the remaining steaks.
14. Lay them on a baking sheet. Coat them with the beaten egg. Cook them in the oven for 24 to 32 min.
15. Allow the beef and mushroom wellingtons to rest for 8 min.
16. Place a skillet over medium heat. Heat in it the steaks drippings. Cook in them the shallots for 3 min.
17. Stir in the vegeatble broth and cook them for 2 to 3 min. Stir in the chicken broth. Simmer them until it reduces to make the salsa.
18. Get a small mixing bowl: Whisk in it the water with cornstarch. Stir it into the pan.
19. Heat them for 6 min until the sauce becomes thick. Serve them warm.
20. Enjoy.

Pan Fried Tofu with Mushroom Gravy

Prep Time: 10 mins
Total Time: 40 mins

Servings per Recipe: 6
Calories   461.9
Fat   38.9 g
Cholesterol   0.0 mg
Sodium   598.8 mg
Carbohydrates   21.1 g
Protein   10.1 g

Ingredients

1 (16 oz.) packages extra firm tofu
Breading
1/2 C. cornstarch
1 tsp salt
1 tsp dried Italian herb seasoning
1 tsp black pepper
1 tsp garlic powder
1/4 tsp cayenne pepper
1/2 C. vegetable oil
Gravy

1 small onion, chopped
2 tbsp olive oil
2 tsp dried rosemary
5 button mushrooms, chopped
1/2 C. vegetable broth
2 tsp cornstarch

Directions

1. Remove the tofu from the water and pat it dry. Cut it into 6 slices.
2. To prepare the crust:
3. Get a shallow mixing bowl: Combine in it the all the crust ingredients.
4. To prepare the gravy:
5. Place a pan over medium heat. Heat in it the oil. Cook in it the onion for 6 min.
6. Stir in the rosemary with mushroom, a pinch of salt and pepper. Cook them for 3 min.
7. Stir in the broth and let them cook for 12 min.
8. Place another pan over medium heat. Heat in it the oil. Roll the tofu slices in the crust mixture.
9. Cook them in the hot oil for 4 to 6 min on each side. Drain the tofu steaks and place them on a serving plate.
10. Spoon over them the mushroom sauce. Serve them warm with some rice.
11. Enjoy.

HOW TO MAKE
Mushroom Pâté

Prep Time: 10 mins
Total Time: 10 mins

Servings per Recipe: 6
Calories   221.6
Fat   21.0g
Cholesterol   62.4mg
Sodium   212.8mg
Carbohydrates   5.1g
Protein   5.1g

Ingredients

4 tbsp butter
16 oz. mushrooms, chopped
2 garlic cloves, chopped
1/3 C. chicken stock

8 oz. cream cheese
1/4 C. scallion, chopped

Directions

1. Place a pan over medium heat. Heat in it 2 tbsp of butter. Cook in it the mushroom with scallions and garlic for 6 min
2. Stir in the stock and cook them over high heat until it reduces by half.
3. Get a blender: Combine in it 2 tbsp of butter with cream cheese. Blend them smooth.
4. Mix in the cooked mushroom mixture and blend them smooth.
5. Add a pinch of salt and pepper then mix them well.
6. Serve your mushroom pate with some bread or veggies.
7. Enjoy.

Sesame Mushroom Stir Fry

Prep Time: 30 mins
Total Time: 30 mins

Servings per Recipe: 4
Calories	240.3
Fat	16.1g
Cholesterol	0.0mg
Sodium	393.7mg
Carbohydrates	17.1g
Protein	11.5g

Ingredients

- 1 tsp cornstarch
- 2 tbsp low sodium soy sauce
- 2 tsp ginger, minced
- 2 tsp Thai chili sauce
- 2 garlic cloves, minced
- 1 tsp sesame oil
- 3 tbsp canola oil, divided
- 1 (14 oz.) packages extra firm tofu, drained and cubed
- 1 lb. bok choy, chopped
- 2 C. sliced shiitake mushrooms

Directions

1. Before you do anything, preheat the oven to 350 F.
2. Get a small mixing bowl: Mix in it 1 tsp of water with cornstarch.
3. Add the soy sauce, ginger, chile sauce, garlic and sesame oil. Mix them well.
4. Place a pan over high heat. Heat in it 1 tbsp of canola oil. Cook in it the tofu for 8 min.
5. Drain it and place it aside. Heat another tbsp of oil in the same pan.
6. Cook in it the bok choy for 5 min. Drain it and place it aside.
7. Cook the mushroom for 3 min in the same pan. Add the tofu with bok choy and soy sauce.
8. Season them with some salt and pepper. Cook them for 2 min then serve them hot with some rice.
9. Enjoy.

CLASSIC
Piccata Chicken with Linguine

Prep Time: 20 mins
Total Time: 35 mins

Servings per Recipe: 4
Calories	562.0
Fat	18.1g
Cholesterol	105.1mg
Sodium	1313.1mg
Carbohydrates	51.9g
Protein	45.6g

Ingredients

4 boneless skinless chicken breasts
1/4 C. flour
1/2 tsp salt
1/2 tsp pepper
1 tbsp butter
1 tbsp olive oil
1 C. mushroom, sliced

1 1/2 C. chicken broth
3 tbsp lemon juice
3 tbsp capers
1 C. parmesan cheese, grated
1/4 C. parsley, minced
8 oz. linguine

Directions

1. Prepare the pasta by following the instructions on the package.
2. Place the chicken breasts between 2 wax sheets. Flatten them until they become 1/4 inch thick.
3. Get a mixing bowl: Stir in it the flour with salt and pepper. Dust in it the chicken breasts.
4. Place a pan over medium heat. Heat in it the oil and butter. Cook in it the chicken breasts for 8 to 9 min on each side.
5. Drain the chicken breasts and place them aside.
6. Stir the mushroom into the same pan and cook them for 3 min.
7. Stir in the rest of the ingredients. Cook them for 6 min until the sauce becomes thick.
8. Add the chicken breasts to the sauce and lower the heat. Let them cook for 3 min.
9. Serve them hot with the pasta. Garnish it with some cheese.
10. Enjoy.

Seattle
Toast (Buttered Bread with Mushrooms)

Prep Time: 15 mins
Total Time: 25 mins

Servings per Recipe: 1
Calories   634.2
Fat   55.8g
Cholesterol   106.8mg
Sodium   615.4mg
Carbohydrates   29.3g
Protein   7.2g

Ingredients

- 4 large flat mushrooms, cleaned and sliced
- 2 oz. butter
- 1 tbsp vegetable oil
- 1 clove garlic, minced
- flat leaf parsley
- salt & ground black pepper
- lemon juice
- 2 slices bread, thick and toasted

Directions

1. Place a pan over medium heat. Heat in it half of the oil and butter. Cook in the mushroom for 3 min.
2. Lower the heat and let them cook for 7 min while stirring them often.
3. Add the garlic and cook them for 1 min. Add the parsley with a pinch of salt and pepper.
4. Heat them for 1 min. Stir in the lemon juice and turn off the heat.
5. Spoon the mushroom into the toasted bread slices. Serve them right away with some sour cream.
6. Enjoy.

CREAMY
Mushroom Boursin

 Prep Time: 5 mins
 Total Time: 35 mins

Servings per Recipe: 6
Calories   154.5
Fat   14.9g
Cholesterol   54.3mg
Sodium   19.0mg
Carbohydrates   3.7g
Protein   3.2g

Ingredients

16 oz. large button mushrooms
1 package boursin cheese, garlic and herb flavored
1 - 1 1/2 C. heavy cream

Directions

1. Place a pan over medium heat. Heat in it the some butter. Cook in it the mushroom with a pinch of salt and pepper for 4 min.
2. Place a heavy saucepan over medium heat. Heat in it the cheese until it melts. Add the cream and stir them well to make the sauce.
3. Stir the sauce into the mushroom then serve it warm with some rice or as a topping.
4. Enjoy.

Twin Cities Style Pizzas

Prep Time: 30 mins
Total Time: 1 hr

Servings per Recipe: 12
Calories   129.9
Fat   9.3g
Cholesterol   21.9mg
Sodium   154.7mg
Carbohydrates   6.1g
Protein   6.0g

Ingredients

- 1 homemade pizza dough
- 8 oz. Fontina cheese, sliced
- 4 C. sweet onions, halved lengthwise and sliced
- 3 tbsp extra virgin olive oil
- 3 C. sliced mushrooms
- 3 garlic cloves, minced
- 2 tsp snipped rosemary
- snipped parsley
- salt and pepper

Directions

1. Before you do anything, preheat the oven to 375 F.
2. Place the pizza dough on a greased baking sheet. Lay over it the cheese slices.
3. Place a pan over medium heat. Heat in it 2 tbsp of oil. Cook in it the onion for 14 to 16 min with the lid on.
4. Remove the lid and let it cook for an extra 8 min. Drain it and place it aside.
5. Heat 1 tbsp of oil in the same pan. Cook in it the mushroom with rosemary, garlic, and a pinch of salt for 6 min
6. Lay the onion over the cheese layer followed by the mushroom mixture. Place the pizza in the oven and let it cook for 26 to 32 min.
7. Allow the pizza to rest for 6 min then serve it.
8. Enjoy.

COUNTRY
White Rice

Prep Time: 5 mins
Total Time: 15 mins

Servings per Recipe: 5
Calories	778.3
Fat	10.2g
Cholesterol	24.4mg
Sodium	80.5mg
Carbohydrates	154.0g
Protein	13.0g

Ingredients

3 C. mixed mushrooms, chopped
1 medium onion, diced
1/4 C. butter
5 C. white rice, cooked

soy sauce
salt & ground black pepper
1/2 C. green onion, sliced

Directions

1. Place a pan over medium heat. Heat in it the butter. Cook in it the mushroom with onion for 6 min.
2. Add the rice, soy sauce, salt, pepper, and green onions. Cook them for 3 min. Serve your rice pan hot.
3. Enjoy.

Beef Stroganoff

Prep Time: 30 mins
Total Time: 50 mins

Servings per Recipe: 4
Calories   924.5
Fat   53.3g
Cholesterol   224.4mg
Sodium   145.9mg
Carbohydrates   74.2g
Protein   37.7g

Ingredients

- 1 1/2 C. canned low sodium beef broth
- 1 (1/2 oz.) package dried porcini mushrooms
- 3 tbsp vegetable oil
- 1/4 C. unsalted butter
- 8 oz. cremini mushrooms, trimmed, cleaned and sliced
- 1 lb. beef tenderloin, strips
- kosher salt
- ground pepper
- 3 tbsp flour
- 1 medium onion, sliced
- 1 tbsp Dijon mustard
- 1 tsp Worcestershire sauce
- 5 tbsp crème fraiche
- 12 oz. egg noodles, cooked
- 2 tbsp chopped parsley

Directions

1. Prepare the noodles by following the instructions on the package.
2. Place a saucepan over medium heat. Stir in it the broth with porcini. Cook them until they start boiling. Turn off the heat and put on the lid. Let them sit for 35 min.
3. Once the time is up, drain the mushroom and chop it. Pour the broth through a fine mesh sieve then place it aside.
4. Place a small pan over medium heat. Heat in it the butter with oil. Cook in it the mushroom for 6 min. Drain it and place it aside.
5. Sprinkle some salt and pepper all over the beef strips. Toss them in flour.
6. Place a skillet over medium heat. heat in it 2 tbsp of oil. Cook in it the beef strips for 1 to 2 min on each side. Drain them and add them to the mushroom.
7. Heat the rest of the butter in the same pan. Cook in it the onion for 5 min.
8. Stir in the strained broth with mustard, Worcestershire sauce, porcini, cremini and beef
9. Cook them until they start simmering. Let them cook for another 2 min.
10. Lower the heat and stir in the crème fraiche. Heat them for few minutes.
11. Serve your mushroom sauce warm with noodles. Enjoy.

GARDEN
Portabella Turkey Burgers

Prep Time: 15 mins
Total Time: 35 mins

Servings per Recipe: 4
Calories   318.8
Fat   7.9g
Cholesterol   75.1mg
Sodium   720.8mg
Carbohydrates   26.2g
Protein   34.3g

Ingredients

1 lb. ground turkey breast
1 tbsp olive oil
6 garlic cloves, peeled
1 red onion, sliced
6 oz. portabella mushrooms, sliced
1 tbsp balsamic vinegar
1 tbsp Dijon mustard
1 tsp dried rosemary, crushed
1 tsp low sodium soy sauce
1/2 tsp salt
1/2 tsp pepper
3 tbsp blue cheese, crumbled
4 sourdough French rolls
salad greens

Directions

1. Before you do anything, preheat the oven grill and grease it.
2. Place a pan over medium heat. Heat in it the oil. Cook in it the garlic for 2 min. Drain it and chop it after it cools down.
3. Heat the rest of the oil in the same pan. Cook in it the tamari sauce with onion for 3 min.
4. Stir in the mushroom and cook them for 6 min. Stir in the balsamic vinegar and cook them for 40 sec.
5. Turn off the heat and let them cool down for a while.
6. Get a mixing bowl: Combine in it the garlic with turkey, mustard, rosemary, salt and pepper.
7. Form the mixture into 4 patties. Place them over the grill and cook them for 5 to 7 min on each side.
8. Transfer the burgers to the bread rolls.
9. Mix the blue cheese into the mushroom mixture. Spoon it over the burgers.
10. Serve your burgers with your favorite toppings.
11. Enjoy.

Bangkok Chicken Pan

Prep Time: 15 mins
Total Time: 30 mins

Servings per Recipe: 4
Calories	336.1
Fat	14.8g
Cholesterol	108.9mg
Sodium	1416.0mg
Carbohydrates	10.6g
Protein	39.4g

Ingredients

- 3 tbsp peanut oil
- 1 onion, cut into slivers
- 6 cloves garlic, minced
- 1 1/2 lbs. boneless skinless chicken breasts, cubed
- 2 tbsp soy sauce
- 2 tbsp chopped gingerroot
- 2 tbsp chopped mint leaves
- 8 shiitake mushrooms, stemmed and sliced
- 5 green onions, chopped
- Thai red chili pepper, slivered
- 2 tbsp rice vinegar
- 1 tsp brown sugar
- 2 tbsp fish sauce
- steamed jasmine rice

Directions

1. Before you do anything, preheat the oven to 350 F.
2. Get a mixing bowl: Whisk in it the vinegar, fish sauce and brown sugar until brown sugar to make the sauce.
3. Place a skillet over medium heat. Heat in it the oil. Cook in it the chicken with onion and garlic for 4 min.
4. Stir in the soy sauce, ginger, mint, mushrooms, green onions, chilies. Let them cook for 5 to 8 min or until they are done.
5. Stir in the sugar sauce. Turn off the heat then serve your sweet chicken and mushroom with some rice.
6. Get a mixing bowl:
7. Enjoy.

Printed in Great Britain
by Amazon